D1739842

SPIRITUAL
REALITY

Transforming the ordinary
into the extraordinary

Lydia A. Mitchell, Ph.D.

BALBOA.
PRESS
A DIVISION OF HAY HOUSE

Copyright © 2018 Lydia A. Mitchell, Ph.D.

All rights reserved. No part of this book may be used or reproduced by any means, graphic, electronic, or mechanical, including photocopying, recording, taping or by any information storage retrieval system without the written permission of the author except in the case of brief quotations embodied in critical articles and reviews.

Balboa Press books may be ordered through booksellers or by contacting:

Balboa Press
A Division of Hay House
1663 Liberty Drive
Bloomington, IN 47403
www.balboapress.com
1 (877) 407-4847

Because of the dynamic nature of the Internet, any web addresses or links contained in this book may have changed since publication and may no longer be valid. The views expressed in this work are solely those of the author and do not necessarily reflect the views of the publisher, and the publisher hereby disclaims any responsibility for them.

The author of this book does not dispense medical advice or prescribe the use of any technique as a form of treatment for physical, emotional, or medical problems without the advice of a physician, either directly or indirectly. The intent of the author is only to offer information of a general nature to help you in your quest for emotional and spiritual well-being. In the event you use any of the information in this book for yourself, which is your constitutional right, the author and the publisher assume no responsibility for your actions.

Any people depicted in stock imagery provided by Getty Images are models, and such images are being used for illustrative purposes only.
Certain stock imagery © Getty Images.

Print information available on the last page.

ISBN: 978-1-9822-0603-1 (sc)
ISBN: 978-1-9822-0602-4 (hc)
ISBN: 978-1-9822-0604-8 (e)

Library of Congress Control Number: 2018906669

Balboa Press rev. date: 06/22/2018

For
my spirit guides,
all the wonderful people who have helped
me along the way in the physical realm,
and my supportive husband.

Table of Contents

Preface

Why I am writing this book? How did I come to be interested in the spiritual aspect of life? What triggered my interest in a world beyond the visible?

To be clear, I am coming from a monistic[1] and omnist[2] point of view. In other words, I believe there is only one stuff in the universe that is divided and created into different forms (monistic belief). I also respect and see that every religion has a purpose and offers some truth (omnist). What I have never been comfortable with is how religions can fight *religious* wars over who is right. The misery and judgment do not seem to be in accordance with the concept of religion or God.

There are many names for the source or creator of all things. I will refer in this book to God as the source of all creation. This word means many things to many people and cultures. I am using it as the name for the divine creator of all things.

Following is some background on how I came to be interested in the spiritual aspects of life—the main events in the path that got me to the current position. It may trigger some recognition in your life of events that shifted your view of the world or could do so now and in the future.

Throughout my life, there were many events that indicated to me we were more than our physical manifestations. The spiritual aspects of life have always drawn me, to the point that when I was in high school, I wanted to become a nun. Obviously, this did not eventuate.

With age, I was distracted by studies and life in general. I did not focus so much on the spiritual aspects of life; the daily activities were enough. After finishing my doctorate in chemistry and continuing on to do a postdoctorate in Denmark, I had a serious health problem. Beforehand, I had been quite healthy. The sickness, which initially came in the form of a terrible flu, was not surprising due to my enthusiasm to work eighty-hour work weeks. At the same time, I was trying to learn Danish.

The traditional medical profession had not been successful in healing me. In fact, I was told there was nothing they could find that was wrong with me. Finally, I looked into alternate health. This was a step out of my box. At the time, I was so unaware of my body that I had no idea one should even drink water. A friend recommended that I see a naturopath. The naturopath took blood samples and examined the cells to see what level of health I had as determined by the shape of my blood cells. He then recommended diet and herbs to heal me. His theory was that the inputs into the body (stress and diet) needed to be balanced by the outputs (the body's ability to clean and restore itself). While resting on the weekends, I had plenty of time to read his book in Danish and roughly translate it. After a month on this regime, I could finally go to work and spend the weekend out of bed. As with others who go through a health crisis, it led me to look at life in a different way. I initially paid more attention to the physical aspects of life, which then became important to maintain the kind of life I wanted, and to work successfully. Once my box opened, I started to be open to seeing the world in a different way.

After Denmark, I did a postdoctorate at the Scripps Research Clinic in California. I was doing yoga one day at home and suddenly felt as if someone had stabbed me in the back. I had a vision of a medieval war situation, and at the same time I was clear it was not an actual physical attack in my home. It was as if I had a sudden memory of an event. This was my first introduction to past-life experiences. I had no idea what else it could be. I was relaxed, safe, and stable. The image, however, was very clear; I could feel the emotions. This is something that I have found with past-life recollections. The emotions were very real even though they were not my emotions in the current framework of my life at the time.

As a scientist, I started to experiment. I asked God for the information as to why I was uncomfortable with a certain upper level manager at work. I wanted to see whether I could solve current concerns with past-life experiences. One day I got a vivid image of a Chinese noble on a horse with soldiers. He had a very bad reputation and was cruel and arrogant. He saw my young grandson and took him. I was a very old woman and poor. I never saw my grandson again. In that life, I never forgave him and hated him with a passion. On seeing this image, I thought I would vomit. I *knew* the manager was the Chinese noble man in a previous life. I was the old grandmother.

Then the doubts came into my mind. How could I know it was him? Where did the feelings come from? Did I make them up? I was ready to stop the whole experiment. But then it occurred to me I needed to trust myself and believe in the information that came to me. If I did not have faith, I would be blocking the experiment before it even started. I could talk myself out of what I was seeing and would never know why I was seeing it. There is a well-known scientific effect in physics known as the observer effect. In this effect, simply observing the object or situation changes the object or situation. According to this theory, one way or the other, I could affect the outcome of my experiment, either by believing or not believing my emotions I decided to have faith that the information given to me was correct, and that my feelings and intuition were correct.

At this time, when asking God for answers to questions on people in my life, I experienced many past-life flashbacks. Sometimes I was a woman, and sometimes I was a man. The emotion was always very strong. This was a characteristic that made me realize the flashbacks were *real*. Sometimes they were a little frightening because the stories were never happy. I was always asking questions in terms of issues I had this lifetime, so the past lives were flashes of fear or anger, usually with unpleasant endings.

Besides the realization that there was more to us than meets the eye, I learned another lesson from that phase in my life. I had been working with a lady in a Japanese lifetime for days, talking to her as if she was there with me in my mind. I could see and hear her in my mind. I told her that she needed to forgive her husband so that I could go on in this lifetime without her background of anger. I had done this work with various characters before. Then it occurred to me that I was talking and interacting with her in this lifetime, and she was responding as if she was there. With this realization came the thought that everything was happening at once—there was no linear time; it is all here and now. The realization was clear and true for me. I have since heard other people talking about the illusion of linear time.³ When I heard this from others, it gave credence to the idea because I'd had the same experience.

I have not done past-life regressions for years. I am not sure whether it was because of the realization that time was not linear or simply that I had done the experiment, learned what I'd needed, and so stopped. I do believe that we have everything in this life that we need to grow and learn. I believe all the issues from past lives that I need to know have been incorporated in this lifetime.

However, these realizations did start me on a rather clear path. It is a path of knowing there is more to our physical world than we choose to see. In the following chapters, I would like to share with you some of my thoughts. The following thoughts and layout have been guided by my spirit guides.

I have been connecting for decades with my guides via applied kinesiology or muscle testing,⁴ which chiropractors often use to determine specific supplement needs by testing the strength or weakness of a muscle; that is where the kinesiology comes in.

Kinesiology studies muscles and their movements, mostly in relation to sports. Kinesiology testing, or muscle testing, has been used as a diagnostic health tool in a number of ways. It accurately accesses our electric system anytime we need to address a physical, emotional, mental or soul-level problem by reading the strength or weakness of our muscles. I had taken a course in California on how to self-muscle test. Healing-with-eft.com gives some visuals of the self-testing techniques.[5] In self-muscle testing, you test the weakness or strength of the fingers on one hand. They will be strong or weak when you ask a yes or no response question. Weak is a no, and strong is a yes. Over a year, I became proficient in self-muscle testing. Since then, I have used this form of testing for supplements, when to go on trips, where to go, what invitations to accept, and anything else with which I needed help.

In California, I studied Feng Shui with Master Louis Audet and then continued on to become a consultant and seminar leader. From my training with Master Louis, I learned the use of the pendulum and dowsing rods, as well as Feng Shui techniques. The pendulum can be a crystal or metal drop form attached to a thin chain that you hold between your fingers in one hand. You ask direct and clear questions with a yes or no answer, and the pendulum responds with a yes or no response depending on the direction or manner it rotates or swings. The dowsing rods which are commonly used to detect water or minerals in the earth, also respond to a yes/no question. You first determine the appropriate direction of movement for the yes/no response to the question for the pendulum and the dowsing rods. The caveat when using these divination techniques is that you need to be hydrated and unattached to the answer you receive. There are many ways to contact spirit or your guides for access to a higher vibrational knowledge. These are the three that I have consistently used.

Well, I was *told* that spiritual reality would be the subject of my book. After soul searching and meditation, I have buckled down and am now fulfilling what I believe is part of my destiny. I certainly hope that you enjoy and benefit from this book. I wish you all the very highest vibration and a smooth ride.

This book is about balancing yourself with the unseen as well as the seen. It is about the effect this balance has not only on you but also on your extended world.

You are transforming the meaning of ordinary into extraordinary.

Introduction

This is a book about perspective. I hope it will help you to think about your life in a new, positive way, giving you ideas about what direction you want to go and what you want to read and focus on in the future. There are many wonderful books on all sorts of subjects that you can delve into. Some of my favorites are *The Secret of Life Wellness* by Inna Segal, *I Can See Clearly Now* by Dr. Wayne W. Dyer, *Magick Mystery & Medicine* by Kristin Madden, *The Attraction Factor* by Joe Vitale, *Type Talk* by Otto Kroeger and Janet M. Thuesen, and *Heal Your Body* by Louise L. Hay.

This book is focused on making your everyday life a spiritual reality and transforming the ordinary into the extraordinary. You're incorporating spirit into your routine, so to speak. We are living in a time when we need to reassert balance in our lives, and with our own balance, we in turn balance the society in which we live.

It is a fast-moving world of microchips. There are many wonderful advantages to technology that we generally enjoy: phones, TV, Internet, cars, and planes. Technology is creating webs of communication around the planet. However, the effect is also to speed up time, with life flowing into a continuous hub of activity. Time becomes compressed, and our emotional and spiritual needs are suppressed. Often with the constant stimulation, we are not even aware anything is missing. But there can be a sense of loss or the feeling that something is not quite right. This may be attributed to material needs or emotional lack in our lives. Even when these needs are met, there often is still something missing.

There is another perspective that shifts the equation of your life, a perspective that brings meaning in to your life. For some, there is a need to focus on a different perspective that is not material or emotional. That perspective can be incorporated into the shifting times and still give meaning and focus to their lives. It is the perspective of spiritual reality, the combining of the spiritual with the physical reality of our lives.

Living a life of spiritual reality helps increase the joy in our lives. Another side effect of spiritual reality is improving one's outlook and hence health. A lot of illnesses are passed off and accepted as *old age*. This acceptance, however, does not help us to learn or understand what our bodies are trying to tell us. We become powerless and lose track of who we really are and how powerful we are.

My goal is to give you ideas on how to transform each moment into a combination and balance of spiritual awareness with the physical world in which you live. With this, the daily chores and work, as well as relating to people, take on a higher energy and understanding. It's a living meditation where your spiritual and physical lives are combined to create an increased balance, focus, and peace.

I would like to start with ideas of spiritual reality and the effect this awareness will have incorporated into your life as a whole unit. I hope this will give you a feeling of what choices you want to make in life and how to get there in a general sense. Some people view spirit and reality as two almost opposing themes. I combine them in this book so that you may do so in your life.

Conditioning has impeded recognition of our spiritual reality until now, resulting in the creation of judgment on many levels. Judgment of ourselves, others, and the events in our life colors our view in a negative way and hence affects our enjoyment of life. We are disappointed when things around us are not what we think they should be. This in turn dulls our lives to the point that it is easy to use quick (and sometimes destructive) fixes to go through life.

Let's start at the beginning.

Think of babies. They are confident and clear on what they want, and they are strong in their communication, although not with words. Babies are full of joy and emotion. They don't second-guess or hesitate when communicating their needs. You may not know what they need sometimes, but when you get it right, they will let you know.

They are basically fresh from the oven. In other words, their souls have just come from the land of spirit to the land of matter. They are sensitive to the environment around them and observant in their own way. They do not have a filter; thought and expression are basically the same thing for them. When they are content and a new person approaches, they go with what they feel emanating from that person. Its only when we begin to filter our thoughts that we can lose our faith.

As they grow older, they need to learn the rules of what we think of as the real world and how to survive in it. They deal with disappointments —for example, they might cry for ten minutes before their needs are met. They might be moved or left alone or with a new person and not understand why. They also become more anchored in the physical world and its conditioning.

As time passes and babies grow up, the spiritual part of their reality is often lost in the survival aspects of their reality. They have less faith, more fear, more awareness of what can go wrong if others are not pleased, and more awareness of the less soothing aspects of life. Hence, with conditioning the separation from spirit begins.

Then we must include in the equation the society in which we live. Its effect is more noticeable as a child grows and interacts with groups and individuals other than immediate family and friends. There is school and then work, and then the computer. The physical draw of life is a strong pull, and the child will leave faith and a sense of spirit behind. There is much to do and many distractions. A sense of fear and uncertainty creeps in—and lots of fun as well, until more and more responsibilities come into play. Eventually, the physical world can take over, and the child does not appear to miss the nonphysical aspects of life that have faded, although he or she may feel a sense of something missing.

In this book, I show how a willingness to find the missing link of spiritual connection can lead to a change in the consequences of your physical world, and how embracing the spiritual in life shifts the need for many less-than-desirable physical learning experiences, with their consequences in the physical reality of life.

In short, incorporating the spiritual aspect into your everyday life shifts both the physical and the spiritual to a higher energy in your being. This spiritual development is dependent on staying in your body as well as reducing the emotional and spiritual leaks that weaken your body and your spirit—loss of energy to other people and things through emotion, fear, illness, or other vulnerabilities. You can reduce emotional energetic leaks by focusing on your body instead of those seeking your reactions and, with them, your energy. Maintaining a healthy body reduces physical energy leaks. Spiritual leaks are due to holes in your aura from drugs, strong negative emotions, and unresolved karmic issues. Being aware of your body and your reactions to the world around you enables you to develop and intertwine the physical and spiritual levels.

When you have the ability to incorporate the spiritual into the physical reality, the boundaries you imagine between the spiritual and physical are reduced. Spiritual reality results in shifting your world into a brighter hue.

You are the center of your universe; you create a weaving around yourself, your friends and family, fun, sadness, and all aspects of your life. You are given personality and challenges when you come into this world. They are not limitations but are things to work with and understand; they do not have to be feared. When you have enough incentive, you can overcome what you might think of as limitations through learning, understanding, and clarity of purpose. Then all the things you have seen as limitations disappear.

Chapter 1

EVERYTHING IS AN AGREEMENT

The following is what I consider the most basic of universal laws on earth. I am not going to sugarcoat it. I will state it and then go on to explain what I mean.

Everything exists by agreement, including our relationships with inanimate objects. This is a basic law. It is often unpleasant to consider because it appears to throw a huge responsibility onto you. In a world where you may already feel you have many responsibilities, it can be overwhelming. However, when examined more closely or in terms of the whole, it really is not that bad.

From a monistic approach (defined in the preface), the concept of connection with all is a given. In other words, you are connected to everything, including the universal source. You made these agreements initially, before taking this form here, and you continue to make them while here on this earth. The overall picture is one of growth and also support from the matrix that is spirit.

You are responsible for your actions but are also supported on all levels by spirit. In the hustle and bustle of life, you may not often see this side of your agreement. This lack of connection with the support you are due as part of the agreement leaves you at a disadvantage. You are not using all the chips you have available to you in the challenges you have chosen for yourself.

In this chapter, I am going to go over some of the more obvious agreements you make with society first, and then I'll move on to the less commonly understood agreements.

Your Agreement with Family, Friends, and Coworkers

With your loved ones, friends, and coworkers, you may be used to the concept of agreement—or disagreement, as the case may be. You may even be used to the idea of agreeing to disagree. For example, when you have a friend who has a different political viewpoint, and you both know neither of you will change your opinion, you might decide to avoid the topic in order to preserve harmony in the relationship. It is a dance that helps you balance in a world of different opinions and varied ideas. With the agreement settled, you basically know where you stand and so tend to feel safer. You have a path you can follow, knowing the parameters around you. You also have an agreement to turn up to work at a specific time, to respect your coworkers, and to generally respect those around you in the society. Hence, these agreements are the foundation of a successful life and society.

Naturally, you occasionally encounter deception or feeling cheated due to lack of agreement. This causes major upsets for people.

Breaking agreements—as when workers do not turn up for work when scheduled, or an employer does not pay on time, or a friend says he will come over and does not let you know his plans have changed—is also upsetting to people. This breaking of an agreement will upset some people more than others depending on their personalities and conditioning, as well as the degree to which the agreement was broken.

Then there are nebulous agreements in which one person thinks the agreement is one thing and the other person thinks it is something else. A spouse may assume that because her partner has picked up the children the last four Wednesdays, this pattern will continue, and she bases her activities around this assumption—only to find that this is not the case. Here again, problems arise. Lack of a clear understanding will, at some point, lead to either revisiting the issues of the agreement or upset and a degree of separation between the parties.

Depending on the issues involved, it can have long-range effects in the life of one or both parties. These long-range effects will then be felt by those around the people involved. In this manner, a ripple can expand from a single nebulous agreement. When the pattern is repeated, it becomes problematic because trust is lost between the parties.

In the case of a dishonest agreement or deception by one or more of the parties involved, the effects are even more dramatic. More ill will and even legal repercussions can result. The ripple effect then goes out to all those connected with the event, and those connected with them are in turn affected by the story in some way. People in the second ripples and those further out will have stories about the situation with their own interpretation, which will be passed on and interpreted in turn. Thus, the agreement or lack thereof spreads. The fact we do not consciously know of all these repercussions does not change them. In fact, the only thing that can change them is a spiritual perspective. Forgiveness is the only solution. The Hawaiian forgiveness ceremony Ho'o pono pono is incredibly powerful and works through a spiritual as well as emotional level. I first learned this from my Feng Shui master, Louis Audet, who learned it from the Hawaiian Kahuna Mornah Simeona. She taught a modernized or western version of healing based on the ancient Hawaiian tradition of the Ho'o pono pono. There is another well-known simpler version now taught by her associate Dr. Hew Len, who worked and trained with her for a number of years which I refer to in chapter 2.

The words *Ho'o pono pono* translates as the process of setting things right. The Hawaiian Kahunas are the equivalent of shamans in other traditions. The word *Kahuna* means literally one who has words and chants to heal. The common meaning for the title Kahuna is *the keeper of the secret.*

For all forms of Ho'o pono pono, there are two main concepts involved.

1) It is based on the belief that all things and people are connected, and that the world around you is a reflection of your own thoughts.
2) The process of forgiveness changes your interactions and karma with those around you.

In the Mornah Simeona Hawaiian process of the ancients, you are forgiving the other person whom you are focusing on, and their friends and family from the beginning of time, for all things that they have done to you. They also forgive you, your family, and your friends from the beginning of time for all the things you have done to them, their friends, and their family. This Hawaiian forgiveness ceremony can take as little time as five minutes when done with intention. The important thing about this is that it is done from your higher self to the other person's higher self. When doing this, your intention is to resolve any issues between you.

There are other versions and viewpoints of this now, as well as books. With good reason, it has become quite popular. I will talk about this in more detail later in chapter 2.

On a personal level, agreement is very important to a sense of stability and well-being, both individually and in society.

Agreements with Society

Social agreements are the foundation on which society is built. All of society is involved. We elect governments, both local and national. School committees help educate our young. The schools have rules to train the young. Parents teach their children rules with which they hope the children will agree.

When you follow rules, they are agreements. They are agreements that have been formalized.

Media-related Agreements

Besides these obvious agreements within the fabric of society, there is a less obvious form of agreement: that between the people who listen to the news and the media who present it. The media seems to influence the beliefs and thoughts of those who listen to it. On the other hand, the news media often indicates that it is presenting what people want to hear.

This would suggest there is an agreement between the media and people listening to it. Keep in mind that to disagree with the news, but at the same time to watch it, is still an agreement with the news media. The watchers are putting faith in the news media to find information they do not have the time, ability, or interest to gather. Whether the viewers agree with the findings or not is another issue – an issue of often great entertainment value between family and friends.

The agreement between the watchers and the providers of the news gives some indication of the focus of the society. When the news repeatedly has stories based on fear and destructive events, this indicates that the society as a whole is fearful, and the individuals feel the need to protect themselves from the rest of society. These individuals are less likely to support society as a whole.

Another scenario is when the news media reports the fear and destruction but also reports on people making a difference in these events and on issues that the society wants to resolve. This indicates a society and people in it that are not as fearful and

5

have the emotional space to work on solving society issues. This willingness is reflected in the news media.

Agreements with Physical Matter

Now we get to the interesting agreements, the agreements with more obvious consequences. The results of breaking agreements with physical matter will be visible, clear, and immediate, not nebulous or slow to come to fruition. Breaking agreements with physical matter has immediate physical results, as I will detail below.

Jumping off a Cliff, Chairs

There are agreements that can be broken without dire physical consequences, and then there are agreements that cannot be broken without obvious consequences!

There is the kind of interaction with the physical world that you, as a normal human being, cannot change at this spiritual level. Society in general has an agreement that physical matter is a solid energy that you interact with in a solid way. You do not interact with physical objects such as wall, desk, footpath, or stove as a combination of atoms with large empty spaces in between them. Society has the belief, and hence reality, that objects and the world around us is a solid physical expression of matter.

You are trained from a very young age that you should be careful of the hot stove, stay away from the cars on the road, and not go near cliffs. In other words, hopefully your parents taught you survival skills. These cautionary notes are very important in a world with consequences. You put your hand accidently on a hot stove, and it will burn. You jump from a cliff, and unless you are a holy master or from another planet, you will die. There are limits to your physical agreements that are dependent on your abilities to handle them and the general belief system of the society. If you were a highly developed spiritual being such as Jesus or Buda you could change these agreements. However, for normal mortal beings, I do not recommend trying it!

These are all agreements you as a human have been trained to make with the solid matter in your world. You would not think to disagree with the pavement if you trip, or with the table you accidently bump into. It is a given that it will hurt you; it is not negotiable. You normally do not argue with these physical realities. The only thing you can do is avoid these situations and take care of your body. At our present level of development, the agreement between solid objects is that they are solid and are potentially dangerous to us.

Then there is the second type of agreement between objects that we have been trained to believe we cannot change—but at times we can. They are less defined and also less dangerous to challenge. In fact, they are often beneficial to us. These are the ones on which I want to concentrate.

What the first group above, of defined agreement with solid matter, taught you is that things are solid in your world and are inanimate. It is unlikely your parents would have approved of a conversation between you and a chair, or their car.

Generally, society considers there to be two basic categories of matter, animate and inanimate. The animate is considered to come in all shapes and sizes and includes animals, man, microorganisms, plants, and insects. These are considered to be alive. People can talk to their horses and dogs without other people thinking they are crazy. The agreement in society is that it is okay to communicate with pets. Nowadays, it is occasionally more acceptable to talk to your plants. This is a little trickier as far as the societal agreement goes. Talking to microorganisms would be considered unagreeable by most people.

The inanimate category includes rocks, water, minerals, shells, metal, plastic, glass, wood, and rubber. These inorganic things are not considered to be alive. Some are fabricated from other components. But the main point I want to make is that they are not considered to have a life force or consciousness because they are not considered to have the spark of life.

The purely physical world view includes the belief that because they are not officially alive, you cannot have an agreement with them. This means that officially, you cannot talk to them. Or you can, but if you hear an answer, you are considered to be in trouble.

Agreement between Physical and Spiritual

We live in a physical world as we see it. It is a belief that we have been trained to have by the society and surroundings to which we are exposed. Hence our experience is limited to this physical reality. However, within this physical framework, there is another level of reality that is subtler and less documented, accepted, or even thought about.

There are many religious groups and wonderful forms of worship around the world, however people often separate their worship from the rest of their lives by going to church (or other religious institutions) only one day a week, or not taking time during the workday or meals to perform a ritual or thanksgiving. The society in general tends to act in the world as either spiritual or physical on a daily basis. In so many belief systems, the physical and spiritual sides of life are seen as remaining separate. There are exceptions to this view, and that is what I would like to address.

The combination of physical and spiritual on a consistent daily basis is acceptable by the majority of the population in movies or martial arts. In martial arts such as chi gong, students are taught to unite their spiritual beings with their physical bodies. In so doing, they perform impressive physical feats such as breaking bricks or boards with their bare hands.

This clear separation between physical and spiritual in your daily lives has robbed you of some of your natural abilities as well as a level of advancement as beings.

I believe that the spirit and the physical do mix and are in fact intertwined. A lot of the healings that are miraculous are derived from the intervention of spirit. In the book *Miracles from Heaven* by Christy Wilson Beam, seven miraculous healings are described that doctors could not explain. There are many Christian references to miraculous healing through prayer. However, before there is any intervention, there needs to be a request as well as an agreement with the soul, subconscious, and body. In other words, the person must be truly committed at all levels for the healing to occur.

For me, a simple but dramatic example of how the body can be controlled by spirit through belief was on Venice Beach in Los Angeles, California. An island man (I do not remember from which island) was performing for people who passed by.[6] The performance consisted of him standing on a chair and jumping on broken glass with bare feet. I could hear glass breaking. He was only wearing shorts. He then proceeded to lie down on the broken glass and ask members of the audience to stand on his chest. I was partly hiding behind my friend as I expected to see cuts and blood. He did not have a scratch on him. Afterward, when people went away, the scientist in me had to ask how he did it and examine the glass (and him) in more detail. When I asked him how he could accomplish this miraculous feat, he said it came from the belief system of the island where he grew up. He said the people there believed that this could be accomplished by anyone. I asked him if he ever got cut. He said he was only cut once, the first time he did the performance, and he showed me a small scar on the edge of his heel. He elaborated on this with the story of how he got started in his job. He explained that on his island, he had a friend who performed this daily but could not do it one night, and so the friend asked him to perform instead. It was accepted where he came from that no harm would come if you did the performance.

After that first performance and one small cut, he had no ill effects. He was a cheery guy who had no issues with his view of the physical world. I could see freshly broken glass from his recent jump and performance. He had indents in his back but no cuts

The point of the story is that he truly believed, and always had, that he could overcome the physical reality of broken glass meeting human flesh. The result was that he could. In other words, there is more at play than the physical body as we have been trained to know it.

Earlier, when I talked of the first level of agreements like jumping off a cliff or a chair, the level of abilities and belief required to survive the experience are on a level of saints or religious deities. At the level of agreement of a belief system about what the human body can do, "spirit" will support that belief. The body will also step up to the plate and do as required. It is an agreement between us and our bodies at this level of ability.

The popular concept of manifesting is another agreement with all that is. You start the manifesting process when you focus on a desire that you have and ask God to bring it into your reality.

- It is important in this process to release attachment for the items in question. It is something that you *want* but not something that you *need*.
- It is also important to take some action in the direction of what you want, even if it is only thinking of it positively or researching it.
- Then be patient with occasional relaxed action.
- When you have your manifestation, be grateful.

Manifesting through your desire, intention, and request is using spiritual beliefs to bring your desires into physical reality. Manifesting is a natural gift that we all have. Some of us are faster and clearer than others, but I believe that whenever you say something or think something with emotion and intent, you are bringing it into focus in the physical plane. This happens even without intending to manifest and so means that negative thoughts can also be manifested in the physical plane. Manifesting is part of the connection and intertwining of the spiritual into the physical reality. Manifesting is an example of the agreement with all that is. I will talk more about manifesting in chapter 5.

Another Level of Agreement: My Cars

I would like to concentrate on the agreement we think we have with solid matter. Our society agreement is that there is no communication with inorganic matter and that it has no life force or spirit. Therefore, it is not reachable or needing to be reached and communicated with.

One day while sitting in my lab office, I started to question this agreement due to the observation I had of a cement wall outside my office window. I saw that the wall had what appeared to be an aura. In this case, it was like a halo of light surrounding the wall. I should mention that when I was young, I saw auras around people, and though I did not know what they were at that age or what they were called, I thought it was normal. Then one day I mentioned it and realized that other people did not see them; it was not in fact normal. After this, I did not see any more auras. They disappeared from my view of the world.

I had started to notice auras on people again at the same time that I noticed the light emanating from the cement wall. Scientifically, it made sense to me because the wall was made up of electrons and nuclei, subatomic particles, just as we are. My work was irradiating these energy levels of the subatomic particles that we are all composed of with radio frequencies. I was working with organic biological solids to determine their structure. In the simple society classification above, they would be described as inanimate, just like the cement wall. In my experiments, the protons in the proteins absorbed energy in a way I could measure with my equipment when I irradiated them with radio frequency waves.

I rationalized the halo on the cement wall based on my scientific experiments, correlating it with the radiation of the subatomic particles that composed the cement. In this case, under certain observed conditions, the halo was evident in the visible spectrum. For a while, I did not think about it, other than the rationalization that connected it with the science I understood and used to describing matter in my experiments.

At some point in time, I started talking to my car. I do believe a lot of people talk to their cars. However, I not only talked to my car, but I demanded and asked that it do certain things for me. I made an agreement with my car that it would never leave me stranded. If it really had to break down, it would do so in a manner that I was safe and not inconvenienced by it. I should say that I also name all my cars. So how did I know I had an agreement with my car? I mentally talked to it in a positive, sincere way, and I asked for its agreement. Then I assumed it was so. The history with my cars seems to verify this. The following are some examples of my luck with my cars.

Since learning to drive at sixteen, I have had ten cars, all secondhand because I do not believe in buying new cars. You may ask, "Why so many cars?" Well, partly because I have moved from country to country and to different locations within a country. Other times, I simply wanted a new model or type.

My cars run well and for a long time without major problems. I have had very little trouble with them. Occasionally I can almost feel when they need mechanical attention or help, and I get it. Once, my steering wheel was shaking a bit, and I worried about it. But my car gave the answer that I could safely wait several weeks to get it seen to, and I was very busy at the time. Several weeks later, I was told that I needed new tires, and that was the reason for the slight steering wheel wobble. I felt a bit foolish because I did not notice the tires; they looked fine to me and certainly were not bald. This fixed the problem. The worst that has happened to all my cars is that I went to start a Subaru in front of a friend's house, and it turned out the cylinders had jammed. It was better to get another car rather than repair the motor. It was an older four-wheel drive, and I had been taking it off-road, which may have had something to do with it.

Then there have been what I consider the two miracle occasions where my cars have lived up to the agreement we had in terms of not leaving me stranded. To date, I have never been stranded by any of my cars. The first occasion after the initial agreement was quite impressive. I had driven by myself up the California coast and was at an isolated rest stop. I had parked the car perpendicular to the curve in front of the bathrooms. The reason for this was that there was a sharp drop-off at the other side of the road and no parking. The road was flat. I locked the car. When I came out, I got a shock: the car was gone. For a moment, I panicked. Then I looked further afield and saw my car parked neatly parallel to the curb on the other side of the road by the drop-off. It had done a ninety-degree turn and parked itself by the curb. I do not know whether or not I had left on the hand break. I would assume not, because it was automatic gearshift and was in park. To this day, I do not know how it got there, but I am extremely grateful for the fact it did not go down the edge or block the road. It would have been a difficult situation given it was an isolated spot, and I was alone.

The second time my car kept to our agreement, I was on the freeway in San Diego. I was in the fast lane. The traffic can be quite busy there, and of course it's very fast. I had a blowout in my tire. That alone was a first, and adding to it the fast lane made me a little nervous. There was enough space in the traffic to move to the slow lane. Right at that spot, there was an exit ramp, and at the end of the exit ramp, there was—you guessed it—a service station. I hobbled to it and got my tire fixed. My car had kept the agreement to keep me safe and not inconvenience me within the limits of its abilities. I was extremely impressed and grateful.

The point of these events for me? They began to clarify in my mind that we can make agreements with inanimate objects. To this day, when I have a problem getting a key in a lock, after about the third try, I ask the key and lock to go in easily. It has never failed. The next try, everything works perfectly. It is not something I do all the time. Really it's more when I need some help from the objects involved. Otherwise, I normally assume that all will be well. This is a very important point, because it is also a form of agreement. The agreement is not formalized as it was in the case of my cars. However, the assumption that all will work out with the equipment is a silent agreement I have between me and specific equipment.

You can also have an effect on inanimate objects without being aware of it. An example of this is a copy machine. Think of the frustrating situation when people are rushed, and the copy machine breaks down just when they need it most. It happens so many times when people are stressed. There are jokes about it. How on earth does the copy machine know we are stressed and rushed? Partly it would be that we make more mistakes when we are rushed. However, I think it is more than this. There can also be an unconscious belief that there will be a problem with the copy machine, which is then manifested. When I am rushed, I have trouble getting a key to turn. Computers can also be resistant in stress situations. It can be that mistakes are made due to stress, and it can also be that we are communicating negatively to the electronics around us, manifesting a breakdown in machine function. These incidences are also a warning to balance ourselves in the physical realm.

Looking at these examples from a higher perspective, I will touch on the beliefs of some religions. Many religions believe that there is a God who is the ultimate creator. This ultimate creator can be seen to manifest itself to humans in multiple forms. I believe the different prophets that have started a religion in different countries are working with humanity on behalf of the ultimate creator. In some cases, the prophets are worshiped rather than the ultimate creator, God.

God is often considered to be formless and simultaneously in every form, defined as pantheism. In this viewpoint, even a cement wall or car contains an aspect of the divine life force. Considering the viewpoint of God energy and the energy contained in all things on a physical level, in terms of their atomic structure, I do believe talking to your car is as not as strange as it would sound. It can be viewed as talking to the God energy within the inanimate object. It is a way of asking for what you want in your life. Do you want a trouble-free ride, or do you want continual problems on the road? It is one way to communicate with the divine in all things and put your case forward at a physical level.

Seeing Auras around Objects

There have been books and articles written on auras,[7] both human and those surrounding objects. Auras are generally viewed as subtle energy fields around bodies. The subtle energy field of auras can also be viewed as the ability of organisms to produce electromagnetic fields. The interaction of electromagnetic impulses with biological systems being described as bioelectomagnetism.[8]

I did my PhD at Carnegie-Mellon University on the study of the molecular structure of a peptide hormone by nuclear magnetic resonance (NMR). Nowadays, a branch of it is most commonly recognized as MRI, where the bioelectromagnetic field of humans is measured for medical purposes. It was this background that made me comfortable with the concept of difficult to measure fields and auras.

Auras have generally been relegated to the esoteric or spiritual. With the event of Kirlian photography, they have been seen by some to have a basis in physical reality. Kirlian photo equipment captures a subtle field of electromagnetic energy that radiates from all living things. In Western religious traditions, it is shown as a halo in paintings surrounding saints. In Eastern religions, it is depicted as energy coming from the chakras or energy centers of the body. There is still debate on the Kirlian photos obtained due to the technique of the electrical coronal discharge itself.

At this point in time, we may not be able to conclusively prove an aura, but on the other hand, science does not have the techniques that are sensitive enough to detect subtle energies on these levels. Even if the equipment was available, the funding would not be. A reality of science is that it always comes down to funding. It is a very expensive business, and so there needs to be a financial payback, at least in the short term. There is also the issue of fashion. In the old days, scientists did the experiments to prove a theory; they were looking into the unknown to find an answer. Now, the experiment basically has to be done before one can get funding, because the funding grants require assurance that the experiment will work and hence the money was well spent. In itself this is not unreasonable. The side effect of this is that the experiments substantiate the belief system of the society that has provided the funding.

Doing something that is not fashionable in the scientific circles of one's discipline will result in a much-reduced probability of obtaining a grant. This makes it hard to advance into the subtler areas of science, which are now referred as pseudoscience.

The long and the short of it is that in the section earlier, where I referred to the aura that I saw, it is also possible that it was the electromagnetic field of the wall.

Either way, I see it not as a scientist, but as someone amazed at the power of life and spirit. The fact that our complex beings produce the bioelectric pattern, whether it is what has been called an aura or bioelectomagnetism, or the random noise of all those nuclei buzzing around, does not matter to me. It is the connection to something greater than ourselves and, yes, to something we at this stage do not understand on a general society or current science level.

Agreement with Our Bodies

Basically put, we have an agreement with our bodies to be here. Each cell of our bodies performs its task to keep us alive without our awareness and very little input. It is an amazing system.

Unfortunately, we do not get a manual about our bodies at school. Most people know very little about their bodies, and because the body generally keeps going, often against great odds, there is no real incentive to spend the time learning more. There is always the backup of going to a doctor and hopefully getting any problem fixed by someone else.

When you become ill, it can be attributed to emotional reasons, food, infection, environmental, conditioning, or stress. It maybe that you have a virus whereas your spouse does not. Your immune system is not coping with the environment it is in for some reason. It can be any one of the factors above. Germs take advantage of a weak system. The input to your body is not supporting its miraculous functioning. The body is meant to regenerate itself. The agreement to survive healthily with your body is breaking down. In some way, shape, or form, you are not holding up your end of the bargain. It could be by not giving it what it needs to complete its normal functioning, or you are sending it negative messages about your life. This lack can be through you focusing on other things such as work stress, family issues, environment, unresolved emotional issues, lack of exercise, lack of water, or insufficient interest in your own needs. It can also be conditioning, such as "I am getting old" or "My mother had this problem." I am not saying that there are not genetic weaknesses in your family line or history. I am saying that they are often used to avoid dealing with issues that could benefit our health and well-being. A genetic weakness does not mean you will have the same problem; it means you have a weakness and need to take greater care of this part of your body than others would. I will talk more about health in chapter 9.

Chi Gong Training

Your agreement with your body is based on your conditioning or belief system. It depends on the society and your family as to whether you have a knowledge base for how to care for your body. People in one country think that the body is limited to certain abilities. In another country, people are comfortable with a whole different set of attributes for the body.

An example of this is a training like chi gong, where the oriental belief system and agreement with their bodies accommodates acts that seem impossible to a traditional Western mind. You may have seen documentaries where a chi gong master will break a large piece of wood with his bare hands. I trained in chi gong many years ago. Part of my training was to hit myself in the stomach with a brick. The idea is to develop the chi in your body to repel the danger and to strengthen your energetic system enough to repel physical threats and improve your overall health.

Chi in the Chinese culture is basically considered to be a vital life force flowing through any living thing. Chi is also referred to as the breath of life that maintains us in this body, and it is observed with acupuncture as a flow of energy. In Chinese, the word *chi* means energy. It is universal energy that goes by many names in different systems such as *Prana* in the Indian culture and *qi* in Japan.

Any physical discipline requires training. The difference in chi gong is that you are training not only your physical body but your energetic body or chi through the physical, breathing control, and visualization process of chi gong.

In the final stages of my training, I could not hit myself hard enough in the stomach with the brick, and so I had to get my six-foot, three-inch husband to do it. I did not get any bruising or ill effects from the process. If your chi is strong enough, and you have trained properly and progressively, no damage results. I stopped the training just before I needed to use a baseball bat on my spine. Some of my friends went on successfully (and healthily) to complete the course. I do not recommend any of these activities without the proper training of your body and chi. The concept behind this training is that when your chi is strong, your body is also healthy and strong.

I mention this as a demonstration of the difference in belief systems and hence training, which can affect your body and agreements with your body.

Mind/Body/Spirit Connection; Energy Work; Miraculous Healings

The mind/body connection has been an expanding area for the last thirty years and is very exciting in terms of adding another component of understanding about how the body works. It is based on an agreement between the body and mind, allowing the mind to affect the body. Conversely, the health of the body also affects the mind. In this sense, there are three levels, mind, body, and spirit, that affect our daily lives.

Miraculous healings are an example of a more versatile agreement with our bodies. The practice of prayer and gestures that elicit divine intervention. There are examples of Philippine psychic surgery faith healing, faith healing in

Argentina and Brazil, and faith healing in other countries in the world. Shamanic healing addresses the spiritual aspect of illness. Shamans believe that illness is evident in the spirit before it appears in the physical body. Thus, healing on the spiritual level can heal the physical body, even preventing the appearance of illness.

For people who have a miraculous healing, their belief system has been side stepped by their desire to heal. They are open to another agreement with their bodies, one that is more important than their belief systems about what the body can do. The healing is only miraculous when viewed from the old conventional belief system. In the case where a healer is involved, they would trust the person enough to make a new agreement with their bodies.

People are healed by many modes: conventional Western medicine, homeopathy, naturopathy, acupuncture, emotional healing, and psychic healing. From these different types of medicine, it can be seen that the body responds to and has a whole range of ways to heal itself, if that is what is needed at the time. I say that because sometimes you need to be sick.

Sometimes there are reasons that you are not aware of, but a part of you may find it more advantageous to be ill. It is hard to judge when you do not know the whole story. It may be something as simple as your body telling you that you need a rest, and so you get the flu because you are not comfortable taking time off work without a reason. It may simply be a bad diet, and your body is crying out for a change. The illness may be a way to shift your life to another level by forcing you to look at alternatives in health and in so doing expanding your view of life.

Or it could be that you had an agreement with God before coming here that you would experience what we call negative illness in order to grow as a soul. If you have not connected with spirit to the level you can determine whether this is so, you are left with the apparent negative consequences unless you look at a deeper spiritual level with the intention of understanding the illness and its connection to your soul development.

Most people are comfortable with the common saying "When it is your time to go, you go." There is an inherent sense that there is more to a long life than living a perfect and safe life. An agreement has been made with God which you cannot recall. There may also be unresolved past life issues that cause illness.

If you choose to change the agreement of health with your body, there are many more options available these days besides those mentioned above. It is wonderful to see the increase in preventative medicine to help heal our bodies and souls before the situation becomes critical.

Examples of Physical Agreements in the World

We have an agreement with the physical world and a belief system that goes with it. It includes useful things like:

- Not passing through a wall when we want to hang a picture.
- Knowing we can sit on a chair and be safe without falling through to the floor.
- Growing food nurtured by the earth, the sky, and the weather patterns.
- Digesting and utilizing the food we eat as a fuel to gain energy for accomplishing the things we want to do in our lives.
- Enjoying the beauty, sights, sounds, and feeling of the physical world around us, including our own bodies and the incredible functions they carry out: our ability to walk, talk, see, dance, run, think, and create.
- Moving from one place to the next in a linear and physical fashion (with a car, bus, train, or plane, or by foot).
- Enjoying the creations we make from a combination of the earth's elements, such as cars, planes, computers, TV, cell phones, art, and quilting.

Summary of Spiritual Aspects of Reality

When your beliefs are clear, you can expand your physical reality to include the spiritual connection you have with the physical world. This expansion will give a new dimension to your physical reality.

- You may not pass your hand through a wall, but you may be more inclined to see it for the transient thing that it is in time and space.
- You sit on the chair and realize it is an agreement with the chair to support you and not break at an inconvenient time. Agreements can then be made with the objects that you use to support you in a way that better serves you. The goal of the objects that we have created is to serve us. If the object does break down—because after all, nothing normally lives forever—it can do so in a way that supports you and your future goals. The beauty of this is that the breakdown of the physical object may be something you needed at the time. Only your investigation of what the event is telling you, and the future circumstances, tell the tale.

   I talked earlier about the photocopy machine breaking down when you were stressed. This is a simple example that can be viewed as your energy being erratic due to stress and hence affecting the electronics of the copy machine. We are electromagnetic beings, and the copy machine depends on a smooth source of electricity. Another way to look at it is a more spiritual approach in which the agreement between the copy machine to work and you to use it is breaking down in order for you to take note that you are stressed and need to slow down. In this way, you become more effective in your work.

   The copy machine is obligingly slowing you down so that you can balance yourself and regroup. It gives you time to do this. Unfortunately, it often has the reverse effect. You do not use the opportunity to balance and relax. You get frustrated at your bad fortune. The next time this happens, thank the copy machine and get some water or calming tea—preferably nothing with caffeine.

A personal example of a different kind was when a friend of mine was not convinced on the subject of communicating with objects. I told him to ask for evidence, and then I forgot about the conversation. We went to a party, and the street was crowded, but there was one parking spot before a driveway. I happily parked there, knowing it was safe and legal. I locked the car and put on the hand brake (even though it was a flat road), and we went to the party. In the middle of the night, we were called out of the party because my car had miraculously moved itself in front of the driveway I had carefully avoided. The police had come to make me move it. The car was still locked! I was quite shocked but moved the car, and there was no problem.

Once the situation was resolved, I started to think about the puzzle of how this could physically happen, and I had an insight. I asked my friend if he had in fact asked for evidence of physical objects responding to us. He looked sheepishly at me and said that he had. I then requested he ask for evidence in a more convenient way next time! My car had certainly made clear to him that he had an effect on it that could not be explained by normal physical responses.

- You can enjoy the creations you make from a combination of the earth's elements. This can be done at a spiritual level, when you start making conscious agreements with the creations to fulfill their tasks in a way that is consistent with what you need. You may be doing this subconsciously in a negative vein, assuming that the technology will be difficult or break down. Likely this is what will happen. I have a friend who always assumes the phone applications will not work. He is always right: for him, they do not work. When he gets tired of asking for help, he approaches the application in a more positive way and is surprised to find that it works.

- A spiritual aspect of growing food nurtured by the earth involves acknowledging everything that created and supported the growth of the food. This includes the nature spirits as well as the earth, the sky, and the farmer involved. When this is done, the food has a higher energy. When you are acknowledged, you shine, and so too does nature.

- Enjoy the beauty, sights, sounds, and feeling of the physical world around you, including your own body and the incredible functions they carry out. This in itself is a spiritual experience. It is acknowledging the beauty of yourself and the earth. The more you focus on this in your moment-to-moment interactions, the more meaning and joy your life will have. Gratitude is a powerful spiritual force.

- You can expand linear time and space to include your intuition, thus connecting you at another level to those people and things around you. You may intuit something about loved ones without talking to them on the phone or physically going to see them. You simply get the feeling you should call them. Or you think about people, and they call you, or you bump into them. Whether you are sending the message or they are is not necessarily important. You have used instantaneous connections through space that you are not used to using, which you call intuition.

One of the most important ways you can develop your intuition is to listen carefully to feelings you may have and trust them. It can be as simple as going to dinner with friends, and the thought comes to you that you should take a wine bottle opener. This happened to me when I started the practice of listening to my intuition. I thought to myself, *Why would I need a wine bottle opener when we are going to a restaurant?* I did not bring it. It turned out to be a small local restaurant that had no liquor license, but you could bring your own wine. My friend asked me if I had a wine bottle opener because the service was very slow. I was sorry I had not listened to my intuition. I am sure I would have impressed my friends, for a start. It was a small thing, but it was a reminder to me to pay attention to the thought or feeling that may suddenly come up. I am not talking of the mind, which wants everything to be ordered and organized in a certain way. I am talking about a feeling that comes up and has a clear message to it. At the time, the message may not make sense, but it is worth paying attention to it and seeing what happens. It is a part of the developing or reawakening spiritual technology.

- Spiritually supporting the creation of a network of government and organizations to help cohabitation and smooth functioning. This is one of the most important areas in which to connect spirit with the physical. Whenever you think of an organization, be it government or the local school council, the thoughts and beliefs you transmit affect the functioning of the organizations. In this sense, it is extremely important to focus energy and transmit thoughts to support a positive outcome for all.

On a personal note, an experience that I had in a research laboratory solidified how effective transmitting positive thoughts to a group can be. The scientists had regular meetings with the head of the division in that area; it was a very large chemical manufacture. The division head was ruthless and extremely rude to the upper management and scientists in the meetings. He often yelled in the meetings and created an unproductive environment. There were two women attending the meeting, and I was one of them. I dreaded going to the meetings, as did the other woman scientist. One day we talked about it and decided to visualize a positive and constructive environment in the meeting. The results were amazing: it was the most civil meeting we had had to date.

I believe the stress the division manager exuded was also bad for him and his health. Within the year, he died of a heart attack while jogging. His body was apparently not happy with the situation either.

Chapter 2

A LEARNING EXPERIENCE

Everything in this world is a learning experience. I am defining a learning experience as an action that has consequences. The consequences can be positive or negative, or even corrective. If there are no consequences to the action, there is no learning. It is rather like the situation of spoiled children: they would keep doing the same thing if there are no consequences to their actions. That is why there are rules for them and deterrents, or consequences, to train them to realize a particular behavior is not condoned by their parents or society. When they go to school, the pattern of consequences is repeated. Hence if they study well and answer the test, they get an A. Or they could fail as a consequence of poor study habits or lack of interest in the subject.

Without these consequences, they would not learn as much in school, fit into society, and eventually be able to obtain a job of their choosing. In the same manner, spiritual lessons have physical consequences in a physical world.

By definition, a learning experience is anything that has a consequence. That is one of the wonderful advantages of our world: you can see the results of your actions and thoughts. This does not mean you have to, or even can, understand or accept the lesson at the time. It may be an experience that you revisit till the light goes on, so to speak, and you decide what in fact the lesson was and whether you will choose a path to resolve it.

In a Purely Physical World

In a purely physical world, there are many consequences. You hit your thumb with a hammer by accident, and it will hurt. You learn to avoid hitting your thumb in future. You do something society as a whole does not approve of, and even if you can avoid consequences for a while, eventually you get caught. The results could be loss of friends or job, or even prison in an extreme case.

Some people do not learn from the results of their actions. This makes it hard for them and those around them. These people are often lost in their stories and beliefs about their lives. They may take to drugs or violence to erase the story in which they believe. The consequences do not matter to them. The internal pain caused by their beliefs in life is harder for them to bear than the consequences of addiction, which they use to avoid the pain inherent in their beliefs. In these cases, it is hard to use the consequences as a method to help them learn. The consequences of addiction and "escape" from their internal pain make it hard for them to consider society and the people in it. They are considered lost souls or crazy. When they are violent, the consequence is a separation from society in order to protect others.

The system of learning by consequences does not work for these people at that point in time. You could say (with plenty of justification) that actions resulting in harm to others are in fact bad or morally wrong when they're avoidable.

In a World Incorporating Spirit

In a spiritual environment, people learn through consequences and also through their own desire to develop and heal. In this case, however, the aware soul is more likely to be in tune with what it can learn from the experience in a positive light. There still is a physical result to its actions in order for it to see another point of view and the full effect of its actions. Events become something to learn from rather than going into fear with regard to the outcome. There is an awareness that you are part of a greater whole and that you are supported on other levels, even if this is not evident in the physical plane. There is also a sense that everything is a learning experience when you take the time, confidence, and faith to examine and understand what it is you are learning as a soul.

A truly stunning example of spiritual development leading to a change in the surrounding physical consequences is the story of Dr. Hew Len,[9,10] who used the Hawaiian forgiveness teaching Ho'o pono pono of the Kahunas to change the fate of inmates in the ward for the criminally insane at the Hawaiian State Hospital. He worked there for three years.

The inmates were so violent that the staff were afraid to go down the corridors; not surprisingly, they had a high absentee rate and staff turnover. When Dr. Hew Len took on the task of helping the sanatorium, he did it on the condition that he not see the inmates, but only worked from an office with files on the history of the inmates. How did he accomplish dramatic healing without seeing the inmates?

Dr. Len believed in the philosophy that in order to change the inmates, he needed to change himself. He believed in taking complete responsibility for everything in his life. Having taken on the position, this meant from his point of view, the inmates were in his world, and so he believed that all their conditions were reflected in some part of himself. In other words, because he wanted to heal the mentally ill, he needed to heal those aspects of himself that they represented. He studied their files. He took responsibility for all that was in his world. He worked at forgiving himself and releasing for himself the conditions each inmate had, and thus he removed the reflections of himself that he did not want in the world around him.

The technique he used to forgive himself was simple: he kept saying, "I'm sorry, please forgive me, thank you, I love you." By loving and forgiving himself, he was changing himself and hence the world around him. Whatever issues he had, he turned over to divinity and asked that they be released. This is an abridged version of the Ho'o pono pono for healing from Kahuna Mornah Simeona.

The words "I'm sorry, please forgive me, thank you, I love you" need to be repeated often and with intention. I have found that the original, expanded Mornah Simeona version, said with intention, does not need to be repeated as often.

When he used this technique after a few months, inmates who had been on heavy medication had their medication reduced, patients were calmer, and the amount of staff absenteeism was reduced. With time, inmates were cured and released. Eventually, all the inmates were healed and released. The facility was closed.

For me, there are three very import points about this story.

1) We are connected to everything that is around us, whether or not we know it.
2) Those people and situations around us are a reflection of a part of us.
3) Forgiving ourselves alone for the components reflected in our environment can release the thread that holds the situation in place.

The following is a personal example of the world being a reflection of who you are. At one point, I was working in a laboratory where part of my job was to train people to use the very expensive equipment that I was in charge of. Once trained, they did their experiments without much interaction on my part. At one point, some new people came to be trained. For some reason, we did not get along well; we even had an argument in the laboratory. It seemed that whenever I looked up, one or more of these people would be in the laboratory, and there was tension in the air (on my part, anyway).

Then one day, I decided I had enough of this situation. Really there was nothing wrong with these people other than we did not get along. I decided to forgive them for anything they may have done, known or unknown to me. I decided there was no issue and no problem. I gave up my stories about how they behaved and what they thought of me, and I let it go at that. After that conscious decision on my part, when they came in, they were friendly. I also observed that they were also rarely there when I was; I hardly noticed them anymore. It was as if they had disappeared. Of course, they had not; it was simply the negative interaction that disappeared, and hence they also physically disappeared from my world to some extent. Apparently, my lesson with them was complete.

My spiritual willingness to let go of the belief and stories in my head about them lead to my change in physical reality with regard to them.

With conscious effort and a clear vision of your goals in physical reality, you can use spiritual techniques to attain those goals. You are learning from the consequences.

Exercise

When you have an argument or are upset with a loved one or friend, practice the Ho'o pono pono.

- Find a quiet spot and recognize that a component of yourself is reflected in the issue about which you were upset.
- There will be stories in your head about how other people are to blame, and yes, their actions can be at fault. But at this point in time, the intention is to release the issue and shift the relationship to a higher, more positive plane.
- Acknowledge that a part of yourself must relate to the other person's behavior; otherwise, it would not be in your experience.

- Then repeat, "I am sorry, please forgive me, thank you, I love you." Ask for divine help to release all negativity you have with regard to this issue.
- Repeat this many times until you feel a shift in your relationship to the other person.

You may find that after this is done, the person in question calls you unexpectedly to talk about the issue you had or to simply move on with other facets of life. The good thing is at this point, with your own internal work accomplished, you will be able to relate to them in a positive way, cleared of the original upset. If need be, you would be able to talk about it in a positive and constructive way.

You can also use the Ho'o pono pono to forgive yourself in both the expanded and short versions.

Blessing the World of Consequences

That there are consequences in this world is a blessing.

1) You can see the results of your daily actions and thoughts.
2) When you develop on an emotional and spiritual level, you can see the results of your work.

From this point of view, everything is a learning experience. You may not like some lessons as much as others, but they are all consequences that you have the privilege of learning from (or not) at that point in time.

When the situation seems bad for economic or personal reasons, take a minute to think about what good could potentially come out of the situation. The experience will shift for the better. Often when there is a bad situation, it is so because you have been reluctant to move on in some way. It may also be showing you that you do not value yourself enough to have what you need to be comfortable at that point in time, or that you do not have belief systems in place that support you.

There are several sayings that come to mind.

If it is not broken, do not fix it. This philosophy leads to pushing a situation till it is unbearable, and then when it is broken, you fix it. Unfortunately, it is usually a lot more traumatic to fix something that is broken than to prevent it from breaking or removing the need for it to break. There is also no control over when it breaks, which usually is at the worst possible time.

An example of this that I have observed is when people do not like their jobs. They hang in there for economic or social reasons but resent the work, and their lives. They often do not feel valued at their jobs, and so they either try too hard or not hard enough to succeed and garner approval. I have found that in the end, their jobs do not like them! With time, if they did not leave willingly, they were made redundant or fired. The situation broke down when they waited and suffered their jobs, hoping to avoid the things that they feared. The waiting and suffering did not delay the inevitable result of their situation. The universe helped them out by getting the employer to do the firing, thus saving them from a job that they did not like or appreciate.

There is also the case in a business of continuing on the same path even though it may be unsuccessful. The head in the sand syndrome applies here as well. It is easier and safer for the business owners to continue on the known path. The known path is usually the path of least resistance. Then there is the final (or second to final) straw: something bad happens that may result in losing the business unless new action is taken. This action can revive the business and help people to decide whether the business (like the job situation above) is something that they want. The bad then becomes good. In some cases, even losing the business could be for the ultimate good. At the time the challenge is to be aware of the long-term benefit or possibilities.

When relationships end, there is a similar process of processing and learning. In such situations, the initial shock and associated emotions come into play before a solution is reached. Once over the hump, so to speak, the sun starts to shine again as you have gained a new awareness and learned what it is you truly want, as well as how to deal with the new situation.

Then there is the issue of violence in the world. This is a very difficult issue emotionally and morally. When a person is raped by another, it is obviously wrong. When a house is burned down on purpose and people are killed by the fire, no matter the justification for setting it in terms of war or revenge, it is wrong on many levels. It is something that humanity recognizes and is generally trying to avoid. In most countries, people have learned quite a lot since the middle ages. It is considerably safer to live in the twentieth century compared to the fifteenth.

There is still violence in the world, which is magnified by the news media and the ability to learn of violent issues throughout the world. These are often the focus of the media, and so each of us has to deal not only with our own lives but also the sadness and violence all over the world, which is brought to us daily. This can be a heavy burden on a subconscious (if not conscious) level. We all die; death is a part of the cycle of life. Given this reality, this aspect of life should not be a shock. This is not to say it is not difficult for you when someone you care for passes. It is a letting go as well as a loss when a person passes on from this plane. It is more the way people die and the intention involved in those connected that is harmful and damaging. A violent passing makes a difficult situation even harder to comprehend and adjust to. It affects the aggressor, the victim, and the observer.

Without a spiritual basis, adjusting to violent crimes and death becomes extremely difficult and may leave emotional scars and fears for the rest of the person's life. This is an important time to connect with God and spiritual viewpoints to give a picture that can make some sense of what is happening, or at the least give enough support to allow a positive path to be visible in the darkness. You do not know what lifetimes have come before and what karma has occurred for the people involved. You do not know what lessons the people involved have come to learn. On a spiritual level, there is much information missing as to why things are occurring on the physical plane.

How can you deal with the physical events and your own lack of knowledge of the complete information on all levels?

I believe one of the most important things you need to learn in this lifetime is forgiveness. Let me say that forgiving something does not mean you are condoning it. On the level of seeing other people's hurt and terror on a personal level, most of your sadness, fear, and upsets are because of a thwarted expectation in other people and their actions, or in the circumstances you have in your lives. For example, when you are angry and fearful upon hearing of a violent robbery, the conclusion you come to is that it should not happen. It is true: it should not happen in a balanced and loving world. The goal of a balanced and loving world is something that happens one step at a time. Each time you can forgive those involved on a spiritual level and then a physical level, you are shifting the energy of the society one step closer to love and harmony, to a society where violence is a rarity. People will still die, and lessons will still be learned.

How do you forgive people involved in creating violence at different levels? We are still learning how to take care of each other and ourselves. In the physical world, as individuals we have several constructive choices on how to deal with this.

- Understand that you do not know the complete picture. You do not know what happened to those involved in past lives and what they had agreed to this lifetime to compensate for past actions.

- Who are you to judge others? Jesus was succinct in this message when he said, "Let those without sin cast the first stone."
- By being angry, sad, and fearful, you are helping to perpetuate the violence that is being expressed in the world. Love does not have room with these emotions present; there is less love and forgiveness in the world because of it. You can forgive and nurture yourself, knowing that this will add to the whole.
- When you accept connection with all that is, you accept that a part of you has similar traits at some level. When you release these traits to spirit and love yourself, you can forgive on a spiritual level those who have done harm in the physical world. This is described in more detail earlier, in the Ho'o pono pono. On a spiritual level, you can work on the characteristics that you have that are reflective of the violence in the world. The Ho'o pono pono is a very powerful technique when done with sincerity and intention.
- On a physical level, help who you can. You can help a group or a person, or even someone in your family who needs it. Help those who need to avoid abusive situations. Another more positive saying is "Every little bit counts."
- You can meditate and visualize on a single goal, with the aim of realizing a higher constructive level for that goal. This could take from minutes to half an hour a day.

This will shift the way your physical world works. Each of us contributes to the whole on a spiritual and physical level.

Chapter 3

RELEASING IMAGINED BOUNDARIES

Boundaries between the physical and spiritual have been instilled in us by our environment and conditioning, which creates our general belief systems. On the other hand, our bodies are inherently connected to all that is by our very physical and spiritual nature.

When you come only from a physical viewpoint in what you do, you only include and see the physical world around you. This is like saying you had a good day because you accomplished everything physically that you wanted to do. But this is often not the case: people can have a bad day even if they accomplish all the physical items on their list.

The physical list does not take into account your mood or if you enjoyed any part of your day. It does not necessarily take into account what brings joy to your soul. You can have a fantastic day accomplishment wise but feel sad and empty at the end of the day, wondering what you had done it all for. You may then wonder why you are not happy with the physical results of your labor. In the final analysis, it feels like a bad day, not a good day. This is often seen as an issue of emotion. But what has driven the emotions? Belief systems that are based on conditioning can be seen to drive the emotions. At a deeper level, I think it is also our spirit calling and warning us of the consequences of our thoughts and emotions in regard to the work day.

When you take the time to do something that feeds your spirit, even if it is only a few minutes or half an hour, you can be content the rest of the day. You have looked after the spiritual aspect in a physical way and can be okay with doing the things you see more as obligations or chores. The obligations have taken on a different color, if you will. They have been blended with your spirit. In this manner, you are transforming the ordinary into the extraordinary.

When only your physical activities are accounted for, an element is missing: the element of your soul and spirit, the energies that drive you to do things. You can say the focus on the physical is because you have to make a living, which generally we all do. On the other hand, because we have to survive and earn our keep, why not do it with something that makes it more than just physical work? When you add spirit into the equation, it changes the end result. It also changes the way you feel about your day and, more important, about yourself.

What does it look like to add spirit into the equation? How can you add spirit into the equation of repeated physical tasks? Taking time out to do something that feeds your spirit can be surprisingly easy. You can think of your own list, which has significance for you. Below are a few general suggestions.

- When you do something out of service at whatever level you choose (see more in chapter 11), you change the task to be something greater than yourself. This is one of the benefits to you by giving yourself a holiday from the little voice in your head that is always wanting something more or is not happy with the way things are. You can focus on someone else or a bigger goal.
- Yoga and meditation are common examples of reaching toward spirit. A few minutes of even one exercise in between your regular work schedule can balance and shift your viewpoint. You can put a timer on for every hour to take a short balancing break. Some people like to start the day out with this to set the mood for the day. It has the advantage of helping your physical body as well.

- Maybe there is something that you love doing, like painting or a creative art. After doing this, your world seems a better place. You do not have to do these things for long time periods; even just planning them can give your day and spirit a lift.

- Pick an oracle card or spirit guide card to give food for thought so you can see the lighter side of life. These are card decks where each card has a special message. You shuffle the deck to give them your energy, and you think about what it is you are interested in resolving or getting insights into. When you randomly pick a card, it will be relevant to your question. Spiritual guidance and your intention will automatically help you select the appropriate card. Try it for fun and see how well it works. There are so many wonderful cards out there now,[11] such as angel cards, Jesus cards, crystal cards, animal totem cards, and spirit guide cards. Have fun with whichever card deck appeals at the moment.

- With a bit of practice and some classes, there are also other ways to connect with spirit. People use the pendulum for yes/no answers to questions they may have, as I mentioned earlier. You first determine a yes or no response from the pendulum, which can be clockwise or anticlockwise, or even parallel to you. Then without attachment to the result, ask a yes/no question and swing the pendulum gently to see whether it responds in a yes or no answer. You also need to be well hydrated when doing this.

- A project that you love and comes from the heart also comes from the spirit. When you want to do something that comes from your gut feeling or heart, rather than your mind and what you think you *should do*, it is a good clue that you are doing something that comes from the spirit. Give yourself time to do it and plan it. Take a break during the day and jot down notes about it. It will enliven your day. Think of your own special, uplifting activity. Simply write down a list without thinking if nothing comes directly to mind.

- If you do not like your job or some situation in your life, you can restrict yourself to ten minutes of brainstorming for plan A, B, or C in order to shift your physical reality. That should help relieve your current stress so long as you do not use it to dig yourself into a negative hole. Only positive thoughts are allowed for troubleshooting!

Being Grateful

Another way to incorporate spirit into your daily life and release imagined boundaries is to be grateful. When you are grateful for being alive and for a million other things, you are acknowledging the spirit in all.

I once asked a friend how he managed to be so calm all the time. He gave me an answer I was rather surprised by. He is a respected school teacher and has a wonderful family and children—in fact, he has what most people would view as a successful life. To my question, he responded that whatever happened that day, he would not go to prison. He had experienced political upheaval in his youth and had seen people go to prison. For him, this was a real, inbuilt fear. He thought of his worst fear and knew that it had not happened and would not happen. Consequently, he was grateful for whatever happened that day. It was one way for him to gain perspective, thinking of the worst that could happen and knowing it would not happen. Everything else that happened to him was gravy. Problems seemed much smaller. He was always grateful.

I give this example not so that you focus on the negative of the worst that can happen, but so that you focus on the positive that you have. For him, this worked.

Think of what makes you grateful to be alive. Be grateful that whatever happened that day, you are who you are, and you're alive to tell the tale. Here is an exercise that may help if you are having trouble thinking of something. In five minutes, write a list of what makes you grateful to be alive, no matter what happens that day. Do not think about it—simply write it. You will likely be surprised with the result.

Communicate Beyond the Norm

When you go beyond the physical expectations that you have been trained in, you start moving into the realm of possibility and open yourself up to new frontiers. Each time you open yourself a little bit more to something that is different from the physical dimension training you have had, you grow a little bit on another level and understand more of the spiritual.

A simple example is when you communicate with your pets, usually dogs and cats. Most pet owners will swear the pet talks back, though there is no physical evidence for this. They communicate through their actions and their eyes. The eyes are often called the windows of the soul.

There was a cute article on BBC about a Seattle girl of eight years who had a different kind of relationship with crows. At four years old, she started feeding them accidently. Then it developed to daily feeding of food and water. The crows were apparently grateful. How did she know? They consistently brought her presents: colored glass, metal balls, and even a screw—anything that could fit into their mouth and be dropped at the feeding point. She even saw a crow washing an item first before depositing it. She faithfully kept all the gifts in packages for many years.

Our cat leaves gifts as well. She is an excellent mouser, but we still feed her more than most cats get. She is active and so is not too fat. She will leave a present of a mouse exactly in the middle in front of the door. The placement could not be more perfect. It is not something I am fond of, but I do appreciate the thought.

There are many such pet stories. It warms the heart and especially makes the owner smile. Animals have a sense of the nonphysical. When you connect with them, you also get a glimpse of another world. I watched a friend's cat track something in the room. It was very intensely observant, as if it was watching a mouse. Visually, there was nothing there that the human eye could see. From this experience, I believe they can track nonphysical entities, or what are commonly referred to as ghosts, as they can physical objects.

Have you ever talked to a tree? There is a whole world out there that supports us and our energy. Some plants give us food, and some plants give us beauty and balance, which helps to make our lives worthwhile. The natural kingdom gives us a sense of peace and tranquility. When we are upset, a walk in a park can soothe our mood and our souls. Next time you see the beauty around you, silently say thanks to all the plants, rocks, crystals, and nature spirits who generate a soothing matrix.

There is an interesting agricultural experiment in Scotland carried out by the Findhorn Foundation.[12] The foundation is based on living in cocreation with the intelligence of nature, where everyday life is guided by the inner voice of spirit. The foundation was started at Findhorn in 1962 by Peter Caddy and Dorothy Maclean, who grew huge plants, herbs, and flowers (most famous are the legendary forty-pound cabbages in the barren sandy soil of the Findhorn Bay Caravan Park) based on connection to the devas and plant spirits. Now there is a community of more than five hundred people who live the vision of creating a better world every day by starting with themselves. They share their learning and way of life in experiential workshops and conferences based on communication with plants.

We can communicate with the nonphysical entities that support and help us through our lives. I am not referring to nonphysical beings who have died but have not left this realm, or ghosts as they are often called. I am referring to spiritual entities who are here specifically to help us on our path. Normally we are not used to the concept of communicating with them on a direct level. We see others who are gifted do so on TV or in the community.

However, we can communicate with them on a simple basis simply by using oracle cards as an intermediary. The answers you get to questions, or even just what is recommended for today, are amazing. You can also use a pendulum and muscle testing. I have a friend who communicates via numbers that she sees throughout the day. She uses the numerological significance to receive her messages and guidance.

These exercises remind you of the nonphysical energies that support you, as well as reinforcing the existence of supportive nonphysical entities. Taking this communication step also gives you the opportunity to thank them for the unseeing help they give you.

In communicating with and acknowledging the nonphysical and spiritual aspects of your existence, you shift who you are. You shift how you feel to incorporate the whole. Your life becomes simpler, happier, and more effective. You also expand your horizons to include the matrix of life.

Seeing the Beauty around You

When you see a beautiful sunset or sunrise, you are awed with its beauty. Even though you may not consciously think it, a part of you recognizes that this beauty is more than just the physical. This nonphysical energy is transmitted to you in the form of peace that emanates from the scene to you thus changing your mood and being.

After all, what is beauty? It means so many different things to different people. But most people will agree that going to a peaceful place in nature is important to their balance. A park or beach is considered beautiful because you come into contact with nature and leave behind the confining rooms and agendas that you have. It gives you a chance to defocus and connect at some level with the spirit that created all that you have.

Seeing the beauty around you shifts your viewpoint. I have been moved to tears by the sight of a deer in the wild; it seemed so incredibly beautiful as it started at me patiently. Seeing the beauty of all around you helps you to let go of the daily issues that are involved in the physical world. When you see a particularly beautiful painting or photograph, it is usually because the artist or photographer has managed to bring forth the spiritual essence of the subject.

This brings you into the spiritual aspects of your world. Seeing beauty is reaching out to spirit and all the wonderful things that have been created. In order to see the beauty in the physical, you need to focus on something beyond the physical and let go of preconceived ideas about what it is you are looking at. See it without the judgments and stories in your head. It is a recognition of the spirit within the physical object that you are looking at. This in turn relieves you of your judgments. Often you are not aware of your judgments and how they affect your interaction with others (and hence your lives). Through your judgments of yourself and others, your world becomes narrow and bland. You lose some of the joy you are able to find in life. We look for easy ways to replace the joy we are missing. Those easy ways are usually addictions to chemicals, drugs, food, games, and doctors.

When you see the beauty around you in terms of the beauty within, it removes the judgment of yourself and others. It gives you a sense of wonder and joy in all of life.

For example, you may have a relative who has characteristics that annoy you for no good reason. It may be the way he talks, or you consider him too negative or positive in his approach with relating to people. When you practice seeing the beauty of the spirit within him on a regular basis, you can simply look at that person and not judge him. You will think to yourself that that is part of who he is, and he has every right to be that way. You will start to look for the things that you enjoy about the person and talk to him accordingly. In other words, you are accentuating the positive. In turn, the person will notice a shift in the way that you approach him, and he may even soften his speech patterns, which may have been defensive in the first place. You never know what transformations will occur in the relationship.

When you see the deeper level of spirit in your surroundings and the people in them, you are less stressed. There are many forms of spirit in your daily life. There is team spirit, school spirit, and people's determination and grit (as in, they have spirit). If you look, you will start to see forms of spirit all around you. From this viewpoint, your emotions are more balanced. You have less need for easy ways of finding relief in a partly stressed and dull life. Your life gains more color and meaning.

When you blur the physical and spiritual boundaries over time and bit by bit, you will begin to see the spirit in all things. This is an inspiring goal because it gives everything you do more depth, joy, and purpose. You have the opportunity as a human being to develop and grow in a way that is not connected to what you do for a livelihood, how many friends you have, or whether others approve of you. It brings you to a level with these external things where, though their effects may not disappear completely, they become less important to your well-being and joy in life. You become more balanced and secure in yourself and the world around you.

Chapter 4

ABOUT MANIFESTING

You want things in life. That is part of the process of life. It is part of your heritage to learn how to attain those things, as well as to learn what it is you want. You have the ability and natural right to create on this plane.

When you manifest, you intend to obtain a physical response to your request to God. You focus on what you want, let go of attachment to it, and take some action to attain it. All of this is done with patience, allowing the universe to supply the manifestation in due time, taking into account other people and circumstances that you cannot know of.

An important point in this process is what it is you intend to manifest. Is it derived from the mind or ego, or is it derived from connection with spirit and divine inspiration? Either way you can manifest, it is usually more satisfying in the long term when it comes from divine inspiration.

In the confusion of surviving, we have lost some of the ability and clarity to create and manifest what we want. You are bombarded with possibilities, and at the same time, through sad and negative media stories, it is insinuated that you do not have the ability or right to manifest. The people in the news stories could not succeed, so why can you? It is important to listen to yourself and what you want to accomplish in life, rather than much of the fear projected in the media.

More and more, we are learning that we do have the power to manifest, and we do have the confidence, clarity, and caring to do so. Manifesting is not only a way to get what it is you want and create a life you want. Manifesting is also a way to connect to the spiritual levels. It makes you aware of how you can access higher levels to create physical manifestations that mean something in your life. In fact, it is a perfect example of spiritual reality. Bringing spirit into physical reality is a very valuable process.

Below is my basic and shortened version on manifesting. I say shortened because there are many books on this subject.[13]

The first thing I want to consider is a question: What is the difference between knowing and declaring in manifesting?

Why would the difference between knowing and declaring be important? The main reason for defining the difference is that in many people's minds, they can seem to be one and the same thing. The way that I use and think of knowing and declaring is as two different concepts. The subtle difference is important, especially when it comes time to consciously manifest your desires.

Declaring

When we declare something, we want it in our lives. For example, *I want a new house.* The declaration does not have to be a verbal statement; it can be a mental connection and request of God. A declaration is important because it indicates that we have made a decision. Before you can do anything, you first have to decide to do it. The age-old example of wanting to lift a book is not the same as lifting the book. At some point, you decide to actually lift the book instead of wanting to lift the book; it is a decision. What triggers that decision is up to you and spirit.

With this in mind, I define *declaring* as a decision you make in your conscious mind due to spiritual, subconscious, and conscious beliefs, depending on the focus you have in your life at the time.

It is important to make a decision and declare what you want, or else you will be left wanting to do it and not doing it. It is the first step in getting to where you want to go.

Knowing

I define knowing as feeling in your being and soul that it is what you want. You have embraced the desire at a level that cannot be argued with by you or anyone else.

It basically just is. It is something that you know and accept as reality. It is a feeling of joy, acceptance, and confidence in this being the correct decision for you and for the highest good for all.

Manifesting Process

There is one thing I would like to point out with regard to manifesting. If you truly want something, you do need to work at some level in the physical plane. It is a physical plane in which we live. For example, sitting on a mountaintop away from the world when you want to manifest entrance to a particular college education will not produce the desired result. You need to physically apply in order to be accepted. In other words, you need to do the physical work of going through the process at an institution that will give you a degree. Similarly, with manifesting a mate, sitting at home meditating may bring the right man miraculously to your door. However, the processes of looking for a partner in a balanced way is likely to have you personally shift to the point the manifestation is something that you are ready for and can recognize. It is not only a matter of taking physical action so that a manifestation can appear, it is also a matter of how the process of acting in alignment with a manifestation changes who you are being.

One other point on manifesting is that I believe it does need to be for the highest good for you and those around you. This is an extremely important point. If it is not for the highest good, you can still get the manifestation, but it can mean that what you manifest does not satisfy you, and the joy you expected to obtain from it could be missing.

Here is a five-step process to manifesting.

1) Decide and declare it is what you want.

Is it a desire coming from your mind and logic, or from what others in the society have? Is it coming from an intuitive connection with spirit? Is it something you feel guided to get or have? Is it something that you feel will help others? Is it a combination of the above?

An example manifestation is wanting to be two dress sizes slimmer. This manifestation helps you because you would be healthier and feel more comfortable in your body. It also helps those around you because you will likely be healthier and more able to help them in whatever way they need, as well as be an inspiration to others to take care of their own health.

Visualization can be included in the process of declaring. If you cannot clearly visualize something, it is unlikely that you can choose or declare it. It does not have to be a verbal declaration unless this is something with which you work better. People use photos if they need extra support in visualizing what they want.

It is also a good idea to write a comprehensive list if it is something like an apartment. A friend wrote a list to manifest an apartment but left out taking pets. She had a cat and was disappointed when the perfect apartment did not take pets. She rewrote her list to include cats and got a great apartment.

It may also be advisable to hold on to your manifestation as a private desire, avoiding naysayers and negative input into your desired manifestation.

When you want to manifest something and are asking for this creation to be supported by God, you likely are affecting other people's lives, whether or not you consciously know it.

Various processes have to be in place for a manifestation. For example, if you want a good car at a cheap price, the person selling the car would also have to be happy with the sale price to make it a win-win situation. How can you be sure that no harm will come from your manifestation?

2) Declare that your manifestation is for the good of all.

An example would be looking more beautiful. You would be asking to look more beautiful and have it be for the benefit of those around you who would see you being happy. We enjoy and are attracted to beauty in its many forms. You are not asking to look more beautiful with the result that others will dislike you or feel uncomfortable around you.

I recommend adding the proviso that it is for the good of all when manifesting. It may be hard to imagine how this would be accomplished because you do not logically know what would be for the good of all. In the same vein, how the manifestation itself comes about may also be hard to comprehend. It is not your job to know all the factors involved and how the universe fits the pieces together. The idea is if the pieces can be fit together for your manifestation, they can also be fit together by the universe for the good of all.

In other words, your manifestation will work out for the best for all those affected by it, whether or not you know those involved. In this manner, you do not have to guess whether your manifestation will negatively affect others. It will be taken care of in the manifestation process.

3) Know that you are manifesting what you want.

You can feel the completed manifestation in your body with certainty. Visualization can also be used in the process of knowing to incorporate it into your being, emotions, and spirit. Again, if you cannot visualize the manifestation in your mind or with the use of photographic images (a couple kissing, a new car, etc.), then at some level you really do not want the manifestation. That aspect would need to be worked on before you could go forward with it.

4) Let go of any attachment to what you want to manifest.

This is often the most difficult aspect of manifesting. In order to let go, you may want to try several techniques or processes.

- Remind yourself that what you want to manifest is not something you need; it is something that you want. This in itself is letting go of a level of attachment to the manifestation. With this comes the realization that you would be able to continue on with your life without the manifestation.
- Then there is the matter of faith and trust. You know that the manifestation is good for you. However, you do not know what form it should take and in fact whether it is something that in the long term would benefit you and your soul's purpose here on earth. It is even more difficult to know on a conscious level whether it is for the good of all. In other words, you do not have all the information at your disposal, but God certainly does. Giving up attachment to

the result enables the result that is best for you to come into fruition.

- You also may not know of the timing for the manifestation to take place in the optimum way when considering all factors. Naturally, you usually have only your time scale in mind. With any manifestation, there are many factors and people involved that need to be in place. This is where you can show patience and not take the delay as a sign to give up. Hence, it is important to let go of the results and leave the final decision to God.

Whatever you want to manifest is for your good and the good of all. When I have let go, it has worked out very well. Usually when I let go, I seem to get what I want to manifest faster.

Manifestations that take longer are those that are solving an issue that has been embedded longer in your being. An example of this is the idea of manifesting a wonderful and loving relationship when you yourself do not feel loved or worthy of love at a deep level. In order to truly know that you can have this relationship in general or with someone specific, you need to let go of a lot of conscious and subconscious issues. Then for the highest and the best, you let go of an issue that may be deeply rooted in your belief system. This is also a form of declaration.

5) Do the necessary physical activities.

In order to have the manifestation appear, you need to be active in the physical world. Getting into a particular social group would involve research on that group. Losing weight would involve learning about an exercising and diet routine that works for you. Finding the perfect apartment would involve looking at ads and clearly writing down your requirements. Do whatever you can physically do to support your manifestation; this sends the message to the universe that you are ready and able to receive the manifestation. To support your manifestation, do these acts with ease and confidence in obtaining the results, as well as with patience.

When these five things are accomplished with sincerity and clarity, you are ready to manifest. You may want to add visualization and any other techniques in enhance the manifestation process.

Be patient with yourself in this process. Understand that you will eventually attain your goal. If it does not manifest at all, look on the bright side: it was a manifestation that was not for the highest and the best, and you are saving yourself from a reality that in the end would not have benefited you. In fact, you will likely be faced with a reality that is a vast improvement on what the manifestation would have been for you. At the time, this is not always seen clearly due to the intense focus of what you would like to happen. You may not be able to conceive of the possibilities beforehand, but you will recognize them when they come into focus. How do I know this? I know this because you have let go for the highest and the best. That means the highest and the best for you. It is a way of protecting yourself from yourself.

Again, it is a process. Some things will manifest faster than others, depending on the timeline of other connections involved and your ability to accept the manifestation.

If a desired manifestation does not appear, you need to ask yourself if you are:

1) Asking for the right thing
2) Asking for reasons that do not support you (e.g., revenge, appearances)
3) Asking for something out of a lack of love for yourself

Patience is a must. I have had to wait one and a half years for a particular manifestation. However, I was patient because I realized it was quite a bit to ask for. I was asking for a dirt road to be sealed, and that involved quite a lot of government money and many people.

I have also manifested equipment in my laboratory. It took a year. As my boss was signing the papers to procure it, he told me that I would never get it (many signatures were required, and it was very expensive equipment). However, I was absolutely certain I would get the equipment, and I did. Unfortunately, it caused a rift between me and my boss. One may wonder whether it was the right thing, or whether I was simply being stubborn. On the other hand, I got an excellent job afterward that I loved, and with even better equipment! Looking at the molecular level of the atoms we are composed of is a rather expense endeavor.

Chapter 5

LOVE MAKES THE WORLD GO AROUND

There is a saying that love makes the world go around. There are movies and books about love. Love has been seen as being connected with the highest frequencies and God energy. There are many forms and many beliefs associated with love.

How does it fit in with our physical reality and modern lifestyle? One way to look at it is through the results of what happens with love. The following are questions to think of as a stream of consciousness type of exercise. You can see what comes to mind for you with each of the questions.

- What do you imagine the results of feeling truly loved would be for you?
- Do you think you would feel happier?
- Would you be more confident and content?
- Would you be healthier and value yourself more because you were loved?
- Would you aspire to greater heights, knowing that you could not lose the love you had?
- Would you be kinder to others?
- Would you judge those around you less?
- Would you be more generous, knowing you were truly loved?
- Would you take care of the body that was loved?
- Would it matter who was giving the love?
- If someone you did not approve of was loving you unconditionally, would it make a difference in your life?

- What if it was a friend you respected?
- If your parents gave you all the love you expected from them, would you behave differently in your life?
- If your partner adored and loved you more than you ever expected you could be loved, would you be content with your life?

I imagine that unconditional love would make a huge difference in your life. At the same time, I am guessing that you would still feel something lacking in your life, even if your parents, partner, and acquaintances showered you with love. Why do I think this? I think this because ultimately you are the only one who counts in terms of the love quota. You are the one who lives your life in your skin with your organs and thoughts. You have your goals and characteristics and karma.

As the saying goes, *no one can die for you,* in the same way that no one but you can live for you or give you the love that you need. And we all do need love.

It is wonderful to get external love and support; it can really help us when we reach low points or difficult times in our lives. However, it is just that, loving support. If we do not love ourselves, we cannot accept the support, and it falls on deaf ears. How can we recognize love when we do not love ourselves? How can we accept a gift that we do not comprehend?

In order to receive from others, we must first love ourselves.

Loving Yourself

Loving yourself unconditionally is what I mean by loving yourself. To truly love yourself, you need to accept who you are and all you have done in life, as well as what you have not done. A key to this acceptance is forgiveness.

Another factor that is important to self-love is to listen to yourself. Take yourself seriously. When you feel or intuit that you need something, give yourself the space to obtain it. When you know you do not want to do something, be honest with those around you. This can be done in a constructive way, explaining how you feel rather than confronting those around you with your needs in an aggressive or defensive manner. You may still decide to do the action, but at least you will have honored yourself and made a choice with the input from others who are involved in the action.

Avoiding confrontation or wanting to please other people is often more important to us than our own integrity and needs. When you're challenged with expressing your opinion or needs, always remember that the way you do it, when coming from love for yourself, is reflected in your tone and way of speaking. This reflection of love will help those around you to understand your case. If they cannot, you can let any disappointment go with the knowledge that they are doing the best that they can and have also the right to be who they are—even though who they are may not be pleasant for you.

When you have a basis of love for yourself, you will not be as dependent on the opinion of others. You are more like a tree taking root than a leaf in the breeze of other people's opinions and needs. This in turn supports other people. You are a constant rather than another uncertainty that they have to deal with in their lives. You have more chance of supporting them, and they will know where they stand with you.

Look internally for approval, not to your spouse or friends or family for love and approval. It has to feel like it comes from you. Every time you are disappointed in someone's reaction or attention, go inward; this means you have not given yourself the feeling of love you are seeking.

When you are angry with a loved one, knowing you love yourself mitigates the anger and gives you clarity and strength. What is even more powerful, given that you already love yourself, is if you love the person as well, you can be both patient and clear. The chances of a win-win are much larger.

If you do not know how love feels in your being, how can you recognize it when it is given and when you are truly giving it? Loving yourself is important to have a sense of what is available. By extension, when you cannot love yourself, you cannot give or receive love from others.

There is also the issue of not being able to give love to others because the well is dry. Sometimes you try too hard to help and support others, draining yourself in the process. This leads to physical problems and burnout. The physical problems are caused by draining one's energy emotionally and physically. In the end, you do no one any good and may even blame the people you were trying to help or please; thus, they become the "victims" of your generosity.

When you can love yourself unconditionally:

- You have learned to forgive yourself for perceived imperfections.
- You have learned to listen to yourself.
- You have learned to respect your own opinion.
- You have learned to express yourself.
- You have learned to acknowledge the attributes you have, as well as the accomplishments in your life.
- You are comfortable with what you are and are not.
- You have learned that your voice matters.

All these things add up to unconditional love and patience for yourself.

Giving Love to Other People

When love is given to newborn babies, it can affect their health and well-being. Similarly, when it is withheld, the babies suffer. Newborn babies[14,15] who were fed and cleaned but not held had more illnesses and emotional problems than those who were held and loved. They are dependent on more than food for their emotional well-being.

When children are loved, they usually grow up confident, and with guiding discipline included, they are caring of others.

New lovers give each other generous amounts of love. When you see people in the first throes of love, it is a wonderful sight. The world is rosy, their partner is perfect, and so are they. All is well with their worlds. If not, a heart-to-heart with the loved one will solve the problem. Perspective will be reestablished, and their worlds will be well again.

Basically, when people are in love, their perspective changes. They see things in a positive light and are grateful for their newfound love. People are more tolerant of others, themselves, and their partners. They love themselves more, reflecting in the glowing love of their partners. Giving love helps them to love themselves.

Similarly, when you love someone else, you can do all these things with respect to them.

- You forgive others for perceived imperfections.
- You learn to listen to what they are truly saying.
- You learn to respect their opinions, even if you do not agree with them.
- You let them express themselves without taking it personally, because it is their issues they are expressing.
- You acknowledge the attributes they have, as well as the accomplishments in their lives.

Remember we are all connected and moving forward in love. Love is for the good of all. Jealousy does not serve you or the other person. Jealousy is a derivative of fear. When there is fear, there is no love. They do not coexist in the same space.

All these things add up to love and patience for those around you.

What Are the Results of a Loving Society?

In a society, love can be reflected more in terms of respect for individuals and differences, support, education, and independence of the society members. For this to happen, the society members themselves would have to respect themselves, as well as other members of the society.

This is harder for me to talk about. There do not seem to be many examples of loving societies, although the egalitarian society of Norway could be on an advancing path.[16] Partly it's because the news media does not focus on this angle. I also think we are developing in the direction of more loving societies, but we are not there yet. I believe it is something that obviously exists, but it is hidden in the fabric of society, and the more dramatic, newsworthy items documented are often a reflection of fear rather than respect, education, and support.

I may be getting into science fiction here with what I view as a society based on love. But then, I like science fiction.

It's just as with an extended family, the members in the society would take care of those that needed help and positive support. There would also be heads of households or states, to help direct and manage the many facets of the society. People at all levels of the society would be accountable for their actions. Those needing more support would get it in order to give them direction and goals to gain confidence in themselves at the level with which they were comfortable. They would also have goals to help build their confidence.

When people are respected and gain confidence in doing things for themselves, society as a whole is a winner.

In general, the foundation for a loving society is evident in many of the world's societies. I would certainly prefer to live in this century than the middle ages. At this point in time, however, the influence of power and money, as well as special interest groups, seems to dominate and receive more press than the constructive aspects of society. With the growth of each individual and his or her increasing ability to support society at some level, the constructive aspects of the society will improve.

You are exposed daily to the notion of romantic love and how you should and should not act because of it. Movies, books, TV, acquaintances, friends, and family give their input. Basically, the idea is that romantic love blossoms and solves all problems. Then you get married, and insecurity, jealousy, and small or large differences of opinion take hold of the love that was once there. This is great for the storylines because there is lots of drama, changing partners, and sometimes an excuse for violence. I am not against this philosophy of novels, as such. It can be entertaining, and one can also learn a lot from what is incorporated in these forms of entertainment. There are also positive, happily-ever-after stories that inspire one to love as well as the psychological aspects of our nature that are often examined and very educational.

For me, the problem is there is no real balance, especially in the visual media. There are movies that are often violent about love, but there are very few inspirational stories about unconditional love, and some of the inspirational movies are tearjerkers.[17]

Sometimes I fear the results on lonely housewives who watch too many soap operas. It occurs to me they may incorporate some of the negative concepts in their own relationships. When one sees affair and divorce depicted often enough, it becomes the yardstick. It seems reasonable to follow the pattern. The concept of working on yourself and then the relationships around you does not seem to come into play. Although the media can be entertaining and also educational, it lacks a balance that is important in our lives. There are of course some excellent movies and series; the above is not a blanket statement for all visual arts.

This balance of unconditional love is not reflected in the media, and so you need to be even more focused when bringing it into your life. When you do that, you will also be bring it bit by bit to a larger part of the planet and the media.

The practice of unconditional love derives from spirit. Bringing unconditional love into our physical reality shifts our relationships, and through them society. When we practice unconditional love of ourselves, family, friends, and society, we are shifting the energy of the spiritual into the physical plane.

The Results of a Loving Planet

When we are all in alignment, the individual, the people, society, and the planet itself will be able to go to higher levels. As a living being, the planet is progressing and growing just as we are progressing and growing.

Our energy is fed into the planet. Whether the energy we give it is positive or negative, creative or destructive, it is fed into the planet. The planet feeds us. As we are becoming aware of now, the many processes in the planet will not be able to continue feeding us if we do not start respecting ourselves and the planet.

When you start to respect yourself, you start to respect others because we are all connected. This in turn makes us more likely to want to survive as a human race on this planet. Not only do you plan for the next job advance or fortune to be made, but you plan for the continued survival of the global population and the planet.

They do not have to be either/or choices. There will be more jobs that focus on beneficial outcomes for the planet and hence the beings dependent on the plant.

When you unconditionally love yourself, you love those things around you. You want to survive with family, friends, a society that works, and a planet that supports you. It is not an indulgence to love yourself. It is not something to feel guilty about when you recognize yourself and the difference you make in the world. Because you *do* make a difference. Like all those pennies add up, all those people add up to a wonderful whole. Individual love grows to the level of society and planetary love.

Is Love an Inherent Characteristic?

People with children will often say that their children come in with different characteristics. Basically, from the time they are born, parents can see the difference in personality between their children. They have the same parents and household, but different personalities.

But do they come in with a sense of responsibility, of right and wrong, or of a sense of loving? As I mentioned in the beginning of this book, I think that children are right out of the oven in terms of their connection with spirit. I would believe that these characteristics are inherent in human beings. They need to be developed, it is true. However, I do not think that the societies of the world would have developed this far without an inherent sense of right and wrong or love in the individuals making up the societies.

We as people have had the ability to destroy other societies and the planet many times over in the last fifty years. We have chipped away at it, but overall, I think the societies are developing in the direction of higher goals for all, rather than Armageddon.

That reminds me of a joke on a Far Side coffee mug that I cannot resist sharing. There were two fishermen in a rowing boat with a big mushroom cloud in the distance behind them. One man smiled at the other man and said, "I'll tell you what this means, Norm—no size restrictions, and screw the limits!"

Oh, to be so positive.

Love in the Realm of Spirit

Unconditional love is usually associated with spirit. We are generally considered too weak or are considered to be sinners, and so we are not capable of unconditional love. Maybe it is the definition, and not us?

We hear about unconditional love in many different forms.

- It is something that parents are expected to have for their children.
- Sometimes it can be used to inspire guilt by others or in ourselves.
- Sometimes it can be used to make us do something that we do not want to do, or we do not think it is appropriate for us.
- It can also be a goal that we wish to attain.

Few people will admit to having unconditional love. It does mean different things to different people. For me, unconditional love is being able to see others and accept who they are, without wanting to change them and without judgment. It is honoring the choices they have made in their lives and for their souls' purpose. We cannot know why they are doing and choosing what they have. It involves letting them make the choices in their lives without judgment.

Helping those you love unconditionally without judgment or feeling sorry for them gives them the freedom to carry out their paths knowing they are loved. You are honoring and empowering them.

There is a saying that you become what you judge. A personal experience with regard to this brought the saying home to me in a loud and clear way. It happened when I was a postdoctoral student in Scripps Research Clinic in California. I had a running partner, and we would run in Torrey Pines along the cliffs paths at lunchtime. He had diabetes and had to inject himself every day. Occasionally we would have lunch after the run, and he would get a hot dog. At this point in my life, I was training for a triathlon and was food conscious. I was horrified that he would eat hot dogs with his medical condition. I was judging his food choices. However, I noticed that I started to crave hot dogs—and I started eating them. I could not understand why until I connected the judgment I had of him and his food choices. To this day, I still have a weakness for hot dogs. So be careful what you judge, because you may end up being just that!

When you help others while judging them, you are loving them conditionally. The condition is that they would be better with your view of how they should be. You are fulfilling your own beliefs and needs. You cannot know what another soul needs to learn and grow. You can simply love them as they are and help them when they indicate that they want the assistance.

Spirit has given us this unconditional love. The greatest gift we have is freedom. We are free to do as we choose. God has let us face the consequences of our choices. We in turn grow and experience life to its fullest. True, we are likely missing some of the information that connects us to spirit, however that will come with our growth and development.

Chapter 6

LIVING MOMENT BY MOMENT

When you live consciously and in the flow of the source of all that is, you are living moment by moment. Why would you want to live moment by moment? What about the future? When we live moment to moment, we are in the present and going into the future. The future becomes the present. How do you plan then? You can plan for the future in the present, moment by moment. Living in the moment is not so much an action as a way of being. Many of us live in the past or the future a large part of the time.

Here are some good reasons to live in the present moment.

1) Forget worries that cannot be handled at the time.
2) Enjoy the details of life that you miss in the intense focus of your activities.
3) Increase your options and awareness by connecting with spirit in the moment.
4) Become more efficient and clearer in what you are doing by defocusing from an issue, thus gaining a clearer perspective.
5) Relax your body and mind.
6) Gain a sense of peace.

Living in the moment may only take a moment, and it may only be for a moment. However, the effect will last for a much longer time. It is like exercising your muscles. The exercise is a short duration, but the effects can last for hours. As with exercise, you also need to build up a pattern and practice daily, even if only for seconds at a time.

Remember that each moment you live is for you. It is your moment. Sometimes you may find your moment is crowd with thoughts of what could be, what could be said, and what you think will happen. When you do this, your moment is lost to these possibilities. It is not your moment anymore. Guard your moments because they are precious.

Here is an example from my personal experience to give you an idea of what I am referring to. I remember one particular morning when I was working in a laboratory. I decided to change my approach to time. There seemed so much to do, and there was so much more I wanted to do. I was always focusing on the next task and the list I had made. This particular morning, I decided that I would simply do the tasks in a way that I felt they needed to be done, without thinking of the next task before I had finished the last one. I also changed the order if I felt it was needed, even though I had originally organized the list in order of importance from a logical point of view.

I started off with the top of the list and continued down. I had an overall idea of what I thought I needed to do. As usual, the list I set myself seemed to be much longer than the time I had available. I concentrated on my goal of going with the flow, moment by moment. I completed the items in a relaxed way and focused on what I was doing. I did not worry in the back of mind about what to do next, or whether I would get it all done (unlikely). I really enjoyed what I was doing and the peace that came from being in the moment, knowing all would be well. At the end of the morning, I was pleasantly surprised to realize I had miraculously finished the list, and I'd enjoyed the experience as well.

You can function in the moment with a peacefulness and certainty. This partly comes from a sense or belief that all will be well. It frees you to actually function better than living in split time zones.

You also enjoy each moment more because you can focus on what you are doing without splitting yourself into different tasks that are ahead or behind you. You do not even have to worry about the success of the task. The mental energy is reduced, and you can concentrate on the pleasure of the task at hand. In this way, you gain a greater sense of satisfaction from your activities.

You are also able to look after your body more by reducing stress and observing any physical needs that come up. When you are in the moment, you are more *in* your body, and so you sense what your body needs. This in turn reduces the stress you are under, leading to better sleeping patterns and a healthier body.

How Can You Live with Mindfulness in the Moment?

Our bodies and feelings are connected to all, seen and unseen. Listening to the mind is listening to chatter. It is based on beliefs and requires a lot of work to eradicate and transform. Focusing on the body and its emotions lets you know where you are at, and it enables a clear connection with the universal energy.

We are all one. It is a matter of releasing the imagined boundaries (see chapter 4). This can only be done from the body-mind connecting to spirit, not from the mind alone. There are also emotions that people refer to, which are a result of the response to belief systems created by conditioning in your mind. Then there are the feelings connected with your intuition and hence the universal energy. I will refer to these feelings as intuition.

Ask Spirit for Help

The first step in living moment by moment is to ask spirit for help. In general, people are very independent. It is often a habit; they are used to looking after themselves. It can also be a reluctance to expose themselves to the negative viewpoints of others. Then there is pride, which is often so well hidden it is not recognized.

Refusing help from spirit can be because you do not know as much as you would like to about spirit. What do you really know of the spirit within all? If you have a religion you believe in, it makes it easier to ask God for the help that you need; he is a set identity. There have usually been generations of belief to call upon.

If you are not connected with a conventional religion that guides you to who God or spirit is, it is left up to you to interpret. When first starting out in a process of connecting with spirit, you may feel uncertain. This can make it a little harder to call on help from spirit because you have not had spirit defined by centuries or years of praying in a religion. You are on your own, in a sense.

You are aiming for a direct connection to spirit, which you need to have faith in and trust is the correct spirit or universal God energy. One way to do this is to always ask for something coming from for the good of all. In this way, you know that the spirit you are connecting with is there to help and not hurt its creations. This protects you and all those around you whom you are seeking to help or influence. In this manner you can be assured that the spirit you are calling upon is for your well-being and the well-being of those around you.

This phrase works because there is a universal law that everything is an agreement. Hence those helpers of spirit that do not agreeing to your terms of for the good of all cannot participate in your request.

Know That Each Moment Counts

Do you feel every moment is a wonderful gift from Spirit? How many moments a day seem like gifts? Would it cover five minutes, an hour, half a day, or all day? What are some of the impediments to receiving this gift? Here are some thoughts on what may deter you from seeing each moment as a gift.

You think you will live forever. You are exposed to a lot of destruction in the news and movies, as well as loved ones who die. It should seem that you would be used to the idea that you will die, and also that it likely will not be a planned death. However, when you hear of death, the reaction of the media and most people is conditioned to be a shocked reaction, as if people should not die. In reality, we will all die; it is simply a matter of how and when. You also cannot judge whether a person's life should have been longer. Of course, you would want to have friends and family on the planet as long as possible. But you are not the judge of their lives and the lessons they are to learn.

I recently read a joke which finished with the statement, "Do not regret growing older. It is a privilege denied to many." I thought that this was a good reminder of our mortality. It also was a reminder to not sweat the small stuff in a society that values youth so highly.

An awareness of death makes life more important. It helps you to make decisions that you may otherwise keep putting off. It helps you to appreciate what you have. Death teaches you to value life, because life is fleeting. Death also gives you a different perspective on life—one that has a larger focus than that in which you get caught up in daily.

The first time I left Australia, I had a holiday in Bali, Indonesia. There was incense in the streets on a daily basis to commemorate a death. It was often associated with cars and motor bicycle accidents. The traffic was frightening. At one point when we were traveling, I realized that we could have an accident, be unceremoniously dumped in a car or truck, and be taken to the hospital, where we would likely be put in the hallway. To me, the chances of survival after an accident seemed slim. What surprised me was that I had never felt so alive. I was aware on a daily basis that it was a privilege.

Unfortunately, as a culture, we live our lives mostly in denial that it will end. Living in the moment is a way to release you from your beliefs and gain a larger perspective by connecting with spirit. It is making every moment in your life count.

Beliefs Hold Your Body Here

Your presence on earth is dependent on your willingness to abide by the general principles of physical reality. As mentioned in chapter 2, you cannot jump off cliffs or crash into hard objects without a consequence. When I talk of the concept of spiritual reality, I am not suggesting that you can fly (some people may, but in general it is unlikely) or do other feats that go against the general laws of our planet. However, you can live in the moment and shift your reality without too much effort. When you do this, the physical reality about you can become magical.

It is like exercising your muscles. In your physical reality, you need to exercise your body to keep the muscles in place and your spines aligned. Your ability to live in the moment also needs to be exercised and practiced to stay in shape. A few seconds or minutes at a time can make a difference. Taking moments out from a task to breathe and defocus helps to reset your moment-by-moment clock. You can then go back to the moments you were in with a fresh start.

Earlier on, I mentioned that your physical body keeps you on earth. A driving force that affects the physical body is your beliefs. In this way, your beliefs hold you on earth. Let me explain this statement.

When you are unhappy, you tend to take actions that reflect a reluctance to enjoy life at best and a clearly destructive behavior at worst. These range from not looking after your physical and emotional needs to addiction and destructive behavior with the consequent loss of friends and health. The end result of the latter is likely to be illness, accidents, and potentially death.

When you have negative beliefs, they are manifested in your environment and hence justify further negative beliefs. This can be a downward spiral. The subconscious effects of this can lead to your body and soul wanting to leave the planet. This subconscious behavior can block positive spiritual energy. Some people's conditioning may not allow even a moment of connection with spirit. In order to gain the imitated feeling of connection, drugs may be taken to live in the moment of bliss. The results of this take a toll on the body and mind, which again go into a negative state of being.

On the other hand, when you have positive beliefs, you enjoy life and are more likely to do things to consciously to stay on the planet. You can connect to spirit in a moment without drugs, simply by being still or defocusing for a few minutes. This experience then reinforces the positive beliefs.

People can change their beliefs in a moment. It is important to live in the moment to avoid the traps your beliefs may set. Each moment can bring a change.

Our Gifts in the Moment

Everything and everyone surrounding you is a gift because you are alive to enjoy it. Also, when you see the beauty within all things, you are uplifted from your own worries and focus. You are exposed to another reality without the heavy judgment that we as human beings tend to favor. You can simply enjoy those around you, giving you another reason to enjoy life and make sure you make the most of it.

How do you do this when you are stressed?

1) Focus on an object to live in the moment.

Watch the object or scene for a few seconds. See the detail in it. Let the belief systems about it and the logical mind take a mini vacation. Simply look at the color, the shape, the light. Relax into the form.

Feel grateful that you are alive and that you have this object to distract you. Watch its movement. With the gratitude comes a sense of the beauty of the object. For a few seconds, it becomes the most beautiful and important thing in your world. You can see the beauty of the object.

Then imagine the objected connected to other objects of its type. If it is a tree, see it connected to other trees. Do you have a message for the tree to give to other trees? If so, mentally say the message to the tree for the other trees. Thank the tree for being there for you. In this way, you are starting to connect to all that is and the spirit in all things.

Do not worry about getting a logical answer or having any expectations of the moment. You are simply being grateful, and in the process you're living in the moment. You are learning to connect to spirit.

2) Breath consciously to live in the moment.

This does not have to be a yoga exercise. It may be that you are breathing in a shallow way. Let that be; simply observe your breathing. It is like focusing on an object. Meditation often starts off this way. Take note of where you are breathing from. Is it your stomach or your chest? Continue to breathe in that way. If you are breathing from your chest, slowly direct your attention to your stomach, raising the lower belly. This allows deeper breathing to open up your lower lungs and allow oxygen to flow from there to the rest of your body. The benefits of deep breathing are many. The breath is the link between the part of our nervous system we can control and the part we cannot control.[18] Deep abdominal breathing encourages the trade of incoming oxygen from the air for outgoing carbon dioxide from your body. It can slow the heartbeat and lower or stabilize blood pressure and reduce the stress response.

For many of us, deep breathing seems unnatural due to daily stress.

When you are in the fight-or-flight response, you tend to breathe in a shallow way only, expanding the ribcage area. This flight-or-fight response is also known as the stress response. It's what the body does as it prepares to confront or avoid danger, and it helps you to rise to many challenges. But trouble starts when this response is constantly provoked by less life-threatening, day-to-day events, such as money or job worries, traffic jams, or relationship problems. The stress response suppresses the immune system, increasing susceptibility to colds and other illnesses, and it increases blood pressure.

Learning to breathe deeply evokes the relaxation response and its associated health benefits of lowered blood pressure, increased health, and relaxation with associated clearer thinking and decision making.

Deep breathing also goes by the names of diaphragmatic breathing, abdominal breathing, belly breathing, and paced respiration.

Here's how to elicit the relaxation response through focus and breathing.

Focus on the object of your choice. Relax, breathe, and focus for as long as you feel comfortable. Start to see the object in terms of colors and shapes. Your breath will follow in time. Let go of everything else except your breathing and the shape of the object.

Several other techniques can help you reduce your response to stress. Focusing your breath helps with nearly all of them.

- Progressive muscle relaxation
- Mindfulness meditation
- Yoga, tai chi, qui gong
- Repetitive prayer
- Guided imagery

3) Roll your eyes to live in the moment.

Yes, that is correct: roll your eyes. Take a moment to roll your eyes. Roll them slowly in a circle, carefully and consciously. When you roll your eyes, you are connecting heaven and earth. You are relaxing the eye muscles, and with it, part of your body. A lot of our stress is held in our eyes. They only get a rest when we sleep or close them to relax. By rolling your eyes, you are releasing stress in your body. Roll them first one way two to three times, then the roll other way. Watch that you are doing it gently and not with impatient stress. Focus on the movement.

Along with conscious breathing and focusing on an object, this allows you to slip into the moment. How long you stay there depends on your experience and how comfortable you are in defocusing from the worries you may have.

4) Use movement to live in the moment.

You may find it easier to live in the moment with movement. This technique depends on the circumstances. I would not recommend this approach in the middle of a conversation or where it would be inappropriate. Shift your focus to your body and simply let it loose! Wiggle a hand, an arm, a leg, or the whole lot at once. Move your body however it wants to move in order to relax and release the tension it is holding.

Do not try to control the movement, other than to avoid injury. It can be ballet, or it can be gibberish. This can be a quick and effective way to focus on the moment. You need do it for only as long as it feels right to you. It may be for thirty seconds, a minute, or longer if need be. See how you feel.

Summary

You can use living in the moment to de-stress and to connect with the spirit in all things. With practice, you will be able to move more easily into a state where you are living in the moment. You can do this for seconds or minutes or a day, with practice.

There was a major shift in my life that was very stressful. It was also the kind of situation that could stress any relationship. In order to cope, I used the technique of living in the moment whenever I felt overwhelmed. It changed everything for me. It sometimes took only five to thirty seconds of defocusing from the worry and then living in the moment to shift my approach to the problem, even when in a meeting on the subject of my stress. I was able to think of pathways to follow in order to alleviate the immediate problem and block out any fears for the future. It was amazing how living in the moment transformed the whole event. In the long term, what seemed like a potential catastrophic event ended up being the best that could have happened.

I recommend that you practice living in the moment with these techniques. You can start by asking for assistance from spirit. Then do one or all of the four techniques. Which technique can depend on the circumstances you are in and how many seconds you have to defocus. The first three techniques work in company; the last two techniques likely need more privacy.

In summary:

1) Ask for help and support from the spirit within
2) View everything you see as a gift
3) Breathe consciously
4) Roll your eyes
5) Move your body intuitively

Living in the moment is an important step to connecting with the spiritual reality around you. Asking for assistance is reaching for the spirit in all things around you, with faith that you are indeed supported.

Chapter 7

YOU HAVE EVERYTHING YOU NEED

In the physical world around you, you have everything you need as a soul to develop and grow. The issues come when you are striving and stressing without balance, because you feel you yourself are lacking. Or perhaps you're lacking some physical wants, which are considered to reflect on who you are. I refer to wants because obviously if you are hungry and need food for survival, that is a different issue. I am talking here about a new TV, car, or bigger house—things more associated with prestige than survival.

You are trained in the physical world to want more. The implication in this is that you do not have enough. There is nothing inherently wrong with wanting more. It is good to strive in life for goals that give you pleasure and help others. Anything that you do will influence other people, contributing to them in some way. There is no profession or job that does not contribute to the world around us. Your soul also has a desire to grow and create, giving you a sense of change and movement.

When you feel you are lacking as a person on a subconscious or conscious level, you tend to want to fill that need with physical as well as emotional needs. Emotional needs would be to feel you do not have enough friends or a partner, overeating, and addictions. The physical toys in effect increase the isolation that you can feel internally. They will never be enough because they are not the real lack in your life; these things are simply a substitute for what is lacking. They are never really satisfying, and so it becomes a cycle of wanting more, getting more, not being satisfied, and wanting more. It drives you to more replacements for the imagined internal lack. With more material and emotional substitutions, it can be even harder to delve into the true internal source of lack.

These feelings of lack are reinforced by the media and ads. When you see events from a more positive light and can find the end good that will emerge from those events, your focus can change. The media promotes fear and helplessness; this creates a lot of conscious and subconscious stress in your life. You can say you are watching the news and thinking, *I'm glad it's not me,* but in reality your emotions are engaged, and it is also affecting you.

We are all connected, and so there really is no escape! When you start to see the bigger picture of spiritual reality, you are less likely to be a victim of the emotional drama and stress of the news media. People are often immobilized by fear or feeling that they cannot make a difference. These feelings carry over into their personal lives. Using your connection with spirit, you are more likely to help support beneficial actions in the world, either directly or through your personal manifestations. At the same time in your life, you are less likely to be negatively affected by the news media

Advertising shows the "perfect" situation that is considered desirable in order to encourage people to buy products. Again, products themselves are not bad. There are many wonderful things to buy nowadays; technology is amazing and will continue to advance. The issue is, will you as a soul advance fast enough to use the technology with moderation? Will you be the master of your toys, or will they master you?

The increasing emphasis on physical objects begs the question: What of the mental and spiritual needs of people? What of the training to develop a happy and balanced person, country, and world?

Those with a strong emphasis on the physical world would like to suggest that with more things, happiness will be attained. The answer is always another toy or drug to make us happy and whole. As long as we do not stop to think and truly feel, this system appears to work. That's provided you do not get ill from the stress of acquiring more and more. The cancer rates as well as other dis-ease rates have increased rapidly and are continuing to do so.[19]

Spiritual Perspective

When we look at the significance of spirit in the physical world, it is a different story. We have enough to be happy and grow. Let me explain. When you see the physical world through a spiritual light, you illuminate many more possibilities of feeling complete without the need for more and more physical toys. You start to see that you have what you need to develop and grow. If you feel incomplete, you can ask for assistance. The assistance can come from a physical as well as spiritual connection of all the things around you. It expands your horizons to see a depth in the world. This depth is not evident in a purely physical interpretation of the world.

You become clearer in what it is you need. When you look around you from a spiritual aspect, it becomes obvious that you have exactly what you need. You can want something else. When you come from a spiritual reality perspective, it is a want that brings pleasure to a being that is coming from completion, rather than from lack. You can develop and grow with what you have in your life as is, or you can have more physical things. You can also expand in a spiritual and material way, coming from your connection with spirit and all that is.

From a spiritual perspective, you have faith that you will get what you need in the physical world when it is appropriate. This faith carries you through times that may appear to be problematic. Take the example of an event not happening. This is a thwarted expectation. Thwarted expectations are usually the biggest upset for people. My experience has consistently been that if I have a thwarted expectation of an event not taking place, it is for the best in the long run.

I had a holiday in Wales that I loved. Traveling by rented car was challenging due to dealing with the traffic, road signs, narrow roads, and roundabouts. I did not have a GPS at the time. My idea of being a tourist is to walk in a park or on the beach and see a few castles and sights.

I decided to branch out and go to Big Pit, an old coal mine. The trip was a disaster. There was hours of congested traffic. Bear in mind that I lived in the quiet Patagonia area of Chile, and I was not used to a lot of traffic. In the end, I was too late to see the Big Pit; I had to drive back with my goal unmet and much frustration.

Then on the way back, I simply let go. I stopped at a lovely, quiet lake with only a few people and pets enjoying the scenery. I realized that I would not make another trip like that on my holiday. I had learned where I wanted to go and what I wanted to do with my time. The hours of frustration and traffic became a constructive learning experience for my holiday. No experience need ever be wasted.

There is always something you can learn about yourself and what you are choosing. Life is a blessing when looked at in this light. Everything and every experience is of value. If you do not like what is happening, transform it into something that you do like. Also, give time and space a chance to transform the situation.

Think about your own life. I am sure you will find many cases where missing out on something resulted in the final analysis to be for the best. This is something you need to remind yourself of when you are upset over thwarted expectations. You never know for sure the real outcome till time has passed. Keeping in mind that what happens to you is for the best and highest in spiritual terms helps bring perspective to missed opportunities.

Creating Your Physical World

You have created what you need on a spiritual, emotional, and physical level. This may be easier to accept depending on your belief system. You may believe you made a pact with spirit before you came here as to which parents you wanted and what life would best suit your developmental needs as a soul. With this viewpoint, it is clear that the situation you are in was designed by you, for you. Having this belief means you truly do have everything you need on all levels.

You have created your physical world in your everyday existence. Every step along your life path, you have made choices, attracted situations to you, and repelled others. You have embraced people and rejected others. Often the choices are the reinforcement of subconscious and conscious belief patterns that you hold. On a spiritual level, karmic lessons can also come into play in your daily life without your awareness of the original reason or agreement for the karmic event. You have masterminded your environment on a physical and spiritual level, and so it must be perfect for you to develop as a soul. In a similar way, your creation in terms of relationships are also the emotional development that you need. When you have learned the lessons your soul needs, you move on and enjoy the fruits of your experiences. You have created your physical world, and so it is perfect for you in the long-term vision of your soul.

The concept that you have no say in what happens to you is something I do not believe in on a spiritual level. I am not saying that you directly arrange every action in your life; some things are easily seen as being attracted to you by your beliefs, and some others may appear to happen out of the blue. They may be past-life karmic events or simply choices to be in a certain place at a certain time, not consciously knowing the consequences of the decision. If you look closely at your thoughts, beliefs, and values, there is an answer for what has happened to you in your life—the good and the bad. There are insights to show you the way to a life that you want. By using these experiences and your spiritual insights and support, you can change what happens to you in the future. This process always involves some sort of letting go. It can be beliefs about other people and the world around you, or a more personal letting go of parts of yourself that attract influences you do not want to repeat.

What lessons do people in sad or abusive physical situations learn? Could their situations really be something from which they develop and grow? Could they find something that their souls needed from those situations? Women in abusive relationships who have overcome the abuse have grown and learned to overcome the fear and abuse, valuing themselves as human beings. When people go through hardship, they come out stronger and more confident. The time of hardship is hard and involves suffering, fear, and pain. The rewards for those who can overcome these are strength, confidence, and often a renewed sense of value in life.

The news is always capturing a heart-wrenching moment of sadness, devastation, or physical violence. You are bombarded with these negative moments in the lives of people around the world. With this, you feel sadness, fear, regret, sympathy, and many other associated feelings, including relief that it is not you. This gives you opportunities to go through the events without the physical consequences. You can learn to be less fearful and more grateful of the life you have, letting go of smaller irritations. You can learn to reach out and support those in need in whatever way you can.

Some religions view suffering as a form of punishment. I believe that God gives us freedom and choice in living our lives, and so I am less likely to believe in outright punishment. I do believe that there are consequences, and that we ourselves punish ourselves on an emotional level and then consequently on a physical level. In fact, I believe we are harder on ourselves than God ever would be. We as a society have also built a strong legal system to punish and control those who have harmed others and the society. This is another form of consequence in this physical world.

All Is as It Should Be

When you come from a viewpoint that all is as it should be, the scenery in your life looks different. It is clearer, relaxed, and more appreciative of what you have. You can see where you want to go. You can appreciate what you have and learn from others. This is a form of declaration. You declare that all is as it should be. As the creator of your life, you are the only one who can declare it so.

With this declaration, you can more forward to observe, enjoy, and learn from your life on a different level.

You can be grateful for coincidences that appear in life and take note of what they are showing you. The coincidences can be as simple as meeting a friend you were thinking about and had not seen for months. Then suddenly, the person is in front of you on a crowded street in the middle of town. It can also be more complex, involving different people and situations. I moved from Australia to San Diego, California. One night I went out with friends and met an old acquaintance from Australia who had recently moved to San Diego. San Diego is a big city a continent away from Australia, and yet we met again and continued our friendship, which had lapsed due to distance and time. The coincidences that can appear in your life are amazing when you start to look for them and appreciate them.

You begin to appreciate that what you need will flow to you, even when you do not directly ask for it. It may be a need that is there, but on a subconscious level. So too with physical objects: they will come to you with time, when you allow it. If a physical object does not manifest, ask yourself whether it is something you really needed. Let go of wanting it and see what happens. Will it come into your sphere, or will you decide that it is something you really did not need now? You still may want that new TV, but on the other hand you can live happily without it. Life is less focused on the physical needs and more on the internal and spiritual needs that bring joy to your life.

This gives you a greater sense of connection rather than isolation, which so much technology fosters. Yes, Facebook connects people, as does the Internet, and they can be wonderful. However, it is a connection devoid of direct human contact and expression. It is hard to look the person in the eyes and see their feelings. There is less likelihood of reading between the lines of a person's response. When you are face-to-face, it is easier to read the energy emanating from a person.

On the other hand, one could argue that in the future, technology will force us to use our intuition and connection with spirit more, in order to go to the heart of the person on the other end of the computer. We will be forced to go to an even greater spiritual understanding in order to bridge the physical and technological distance.

Chapter 8

LIVING WELL IN YOUR BODY

In this chapter, I would like to talk about taking care of the physical vehicle that keeps us physically here on earth: our bodies. When our bodies are healthy, it is much easier to have a full and enjoyable life. Our physical health affects our mental and emotional health, and hence our ability to reach for the level of spiritual connection. Going to the doctor is expensive in terms of the stress factor, time, and money. It distracts from other more constructive pursuits in life and is something best avoided. The effort you take in looking after your physical vessel is well worth it in the short and long term. We are not given a manual on how to look after and nourish our bodies at school. A manual would be handy, both for the physical and emotion aspects of our being.

This chapter is not a manual, but it may give you some ideas to try. Each body is different. Connecting with your intuition, body, and spirit is a wonderful way to gain confidence in looking after your body.

Spiritual Connection to Your Food

The pace of life is increasing, and survival is being measured more in economic terms than the basic survival instincts of our ancestors. With this shift, we have lost some of the enjoyment in food and drink. Often it is a matter of gulping something down so we can do something else. We have so much food available in developed countries that we need to stimulate jaded palates more and more. The meal needs to have many components to deserve our attention, let alone our praise. The idea of sitting down and enjoying a simple vegetable without an abundance of addictive fat and sugar does generally not appeal to us. Also, the idea of eating one item is very rare. Our stomachs get many and sometimes conflicting ingredients to digest—starches with protein, for example. We manage to break down the food to some level, because we are incredibly adaptable.

You may be so busy and focused that you do not notice the consequences to your health and body till you are ill. When you do have time away from work, it is often spent recovering in front of the TV because you are too tired from working and emotional stress to use extra energy on thinking about your health. You may not become physically ill to the level of incapacitation, but you may put on weight or find you cannot climb the stairs easily anymore. You may find yourself getting more despondent and depressed, or forgetting things more easily. These signs, left unnoticed with time, add up to affect your health in a negative way.

"If it is not broken, do not fix it" is often the motto. People tend to wait until their bodies have broken down in some form, and then they go to the doctor. It is believed that is what doctors are for, a quick fix. They can hopefully alleviate the symptoms your body is producing, but normally they are not able to remove the actual cause of the symptoms. This results in more symptoms and sometimes reactions to the drugs used to remove the symptoms. Learning about our bodies and preventive medicine takes time, which we often feel we do not have. Unfortunately, time is all we really have, and our bodies are the vehicle of that time. When they run out, so do we.

We are losing the connection and appreciation of our food. We are also losing the connection with our bodies that keeps us alive and gives us time. Looked at in another way, when you lose connection with your body, you lose connection with the vehicle that connects you to spirit. The instinct to eat what your body needs has almost been lost. Now you have to be told what you need to eat. Do you have to tell and animal what it can and cannot eat? When a lion hunts, it knows that it hunts for meat. A lion will eat till it's full, and then it'll stop even if there is food left. It will not hunt again for days till it is hungry. It listens to its body irrespective of how much food is available. It does not clean its plate when its stomach is already full.

Animals will usually leave poisonous food even when they are hungry. Pets, on the other hand, have often followed in their masters' footsteps, and hence they have obesity and health issues as well.

When you respect your food and connect with it, you are ensuring your own survival. Often in the rush to the top, you forget that your body is the temple that houses your soul. Without your body, you die, and the soul that keeps you alive has no place to go. That spark of life is lost on this earth.

If you want to enjoy life in a healthier state and for longer, you need to counteract the pull of an overoccupied life. You all know people who are sick. More and more are getting sick. We are living longer overall, but is it a life that we want? Can we afford it financially and emotionally?

The simple ceremony I am going to recommend carrying out before a meal could take seconds. However, it can bring your spirit, body, and food back into balance.

1) Take a minute to look at your plate and the food on it. This also gets your digestive juices ready to go!
2) Say a blessing of gratitude for the food. One of my favorite blessings is, "Bless this food and all those connected with it."
3) Think of something positive that you are grateful for in your life. Say that to yourself or the people at the table.
4) Know that the food brings you health and joy.

5) Ask the food to be easily absorbed and digested by your digestive system, giving you the nutrients that you need. Also ask that those components that you cannot use pass easily through your system with no damage to your system. (This is assuming you are not allergic to anything on your plate—in which case you should not be eating it!)

By requesting this of the food, you are making an agreement with the food (see chapter 1 on agreement). If you get a strong no to the request, scan the plate to see what particular food is causing the no, and do not eat that food. You can scan the plate by looking at each category of food on the plate and asking it if it will pass through your digestive system without harming you.

When you say the blessing, you can think of the earth and elements that nurtured the food source. Then there are the nature spirits, farmer, trucker, and market workers, as well as the person who prepared the meal and those sitting at the table together to enjoy the meal with each other. The words "all those connected with it" covers a lot of ground. It makes you very grateful for the process and effort that brought the food to your plate.

You may already have your own blessing, or you can make your own blessings to give your meal a spiritual significance. The thought of gratitude for something in your life will bring greater significance to both your food and your life.

Your food is giving you life and connecting you to spirit and all the miracles of life. When you acknowledge the food you eat, you recognize these miracles.

Your body is an amazing creation that is masterminded by your brain, emotions, and conditioned belief systems. It does what you tell it to without question. The question is, do you know what to tell it to do? Do you know what to ask your incredibly intelligent body? I am adding to the list.

6) Ask the food if you should eat it, and how much of it. Feel how it would be in your body after you have eaten it. Listen to the answers and how you truly feel.

When you are asking the food if you should eat it, you are in effect asking yourself. You do this via your connection to the spirit in all things.

Lifestyle and Food

In our modern society, our immune systems are failing to keep up. This has resulted in a higher incidence of autoimmune diseases. The increased levels of cancer reflect the inability of our immune system to keep up with the usual cancer cell–cleaning task. We always have cancer cells present, but disease results when the body cannot cope and is unable to remove these cells.

I believe these increases in autoimmune and inflammatory diseases are being seen due to the combination of emotional and physical factors listed below. They are not in order and will affect each person differently.

- Stress associated with the fast pace of life
- Unresolved emotional or spiritual issues
- Insufficient exercise
- Low joy quota
- Increased electromagnetic pollution slowly eroding the immune system
- Lack of healthy gut microorganisms
- Poor internal hygiene, with resulting internal buildup of toxins in the body

Then There Is Exercise

How do you incorporate spirit into exercise? When you exercise, you support your body and hence your soul. When you are healthy, you help those around you to be healthy. They may not exercise as you do, but they have a positive example in their lives: you. You will be healthier because of it and so give off a different kind of energy as well.

Exercising can also be a form of meditation. It is time for you. It is a time to let thoughts flow from spirit, to just be. The routine becomes a form of meditation. Instead of mulling over a problem that you think you have, it is good to simply let go and see the thoughts floating away. Start to observe what is around you, whether it is a wall or a tree. Have that be your focus for a while. Ask spirit to help you in whatever you need support for. You will soon see other thoughts coming to you that help with concerns in your life. It may also be the awareness of the beauty around you.

Practically, my philosophy on exercise is "Anything is better than nothing." There are several sayings I go by:

The older you get, the more maintenance. Rather like a car!

If you do not use it, you lose it! Sometimes I only exercise for ten to fifteen minutes per day. However, this gives my body the idea that I am interested in my relationship with it, and it knows it has to keep going.

If you are having a hard time motivating yourself to exercise, you can exercise for a cause greater than yourself. It could be a broad cause (for the good of all) or a narrow cause (for my neighbor's children, who need to see a good role model for exercising and taking care of one's health). It can be something that calls to you and that you want to support. Each exercise you do will give energy to your declared cause. It is like a physical donation of sorts. The energy is transmitted to your declared cause through the connection of all that is. You also have the benefit of more incentive to work out. I have found that it also makes the physical activity easier, with less likelihood of being focused on simply getting the next exercise done. It becomes a form of focused meditation.

The main thing with exercise is to do something that you enjoy.

- If you are a social person, take a class.
- If you do not have time for a fixed schedule to exercise, watch a video, or go running or walking.
- I am also a big fan of short exercise breaks, a stretch here and there, and a few squats to get the circulation going.
- In an office, you can do one stretching exercise during your break.
- For traveling, exercise bands are light.
- Another favorite is to simply dance to your own mental music for a few minutes. This takes a lot of energy as well as releasing stress.
- Yoga is excellent for stretching. Kundalini yoga is a favorite of mine because it has more movement and so is easier than longer standing poses.
- Social sports outside are great—hiking, golfing, bicycling, swimming, and boating.
- Arrange a walk schedule with friends, supporting both of you.

Always listen to your body. Know that it does not have to be a chore of an hour out of your day. Just get your body moving!

Simple Diet Suggestions

The following are simple dietary suggestions to maintain a healthy body. There are many more, however I would like to keep it simple. You should always go with your gut or the talk you have with your food. The following list is a minimum to make it simple and get you started on a healthy path. Basically, all natural (as opposed to processed) food will benefit you in some way. The exception is if you are intolerant of the food, overeat, or eat too much food that's incompatible with your blood type (see Dr. D'Adamo's work[20]).

Some Recommended Foods:

- Beetroot, lightly cooked or raw: It's great for the liver and is a source of betalains. It has been shown to provide antioxidant, anti-inflammatory, and detoxification support.
- Celery: A good source of potassium, sodium, calcium, manganese, and magnesium. Potassium is an important component of cell and body fluids that helps regulate heart rate and blood pressure. Celery is an excellent source of vitamin K, which helps increase bone mass. Celery is also rich in many vital vitamins: vitamin A, folic acid, riboflavin, niacin, and vitamin C, which are essential for optimum metabolism.
- Parsley: Made into a tea, it is great for the kidneys. It is a vitamin C–rich food that provides protection against inflammatory polyarthritis, a form of rheumatoid arthritis involving two or more joints. There is a high folic acid content in parsley for heart health and cancer prevention.
- Apples: They are high in fiber and vitamin C, and they're high in polyphenols, which function as antioxidants and can help regulate blood sugar. They are good for the prevention of heart disease through healthy regulation of blood fat levels. Apples are magic for the digestive system due to their support and their positive impact on bacteria in the digestive tract.
- Almonds: They are alkalinizing and are rich in monounsaturated fatty acids like oleic, which that help in lowering LDL or "bad cholesterol." They contain vitamin E and vitamin B complex vitamins and minerals.
- Fish: It is food for the brain and eyes due to the omega-3 fatty acids, as well as good protein. It also provides vitamins A and D, phosphorus, magnesium, selenium, and iodine (in marine fish).
- Turmeric root is shown to be anti-cancer and anti-inflammation for all blood types.

Two Recommended Drinks

Water is the giver of life, and although body weight varies with age and sex, the percentage of water to body weight is approximately 65 percent[21] for adults. The human brain is about 85 percent water, and the bones are between 10–15 percent water.

Often, you think you are hungry, but you are thirsty. If you tend to drink dehydrating drinks like tea, coffee, and sugary drinks, you are losing more water in the process of hydrating.

The lack of water in our bodies causes the spinal disks to dehydrate, with consequent slipping and fracturing. It also causes our skin to dry out as well. There are many reasons to make sure you get enough water for your body processes to function. Every system in your body depends on water. Even mild dehydration can drain your energy, make you tired, and affect your clarity of mind. Water is also important for digestion and good bowel function. I do not recommend water with meals; rather drink it before or an hour after meals so that the digestive enzymes can do their work.

If you do not like to drink straight water, add a little lemon juice to the water, or place a slice of apple or lemon in the water to improve the taste.

Recommendations vary from eight to ten glasses per day (pregnancy requires more water) for women, and thirteen glasses for men. If it is very hot or you exercise a lot, you will need more.

Can you drink too much? If you drink over four liters and are not an athlete, it likely is too much.

Vegetable juices are an excellent way to alkalize your body and get some good vitamins and minerals. My favorite is carrot, beet, celery, and a clove of garlic. I also recommend a green juice of spinach or swiss chard with half to a whole lemon and an apple to help the flavor and digestion.

The downside of vegetable juices is that they generally lack fiber, which is needed in your diet for good bowel function and to feed the enterobacterium in the intestines.

On Fats

Fats and sugars are addictive substances, so they are something to watch out for. Carbohydrates from white bread and pasta are a form of sugar when broken down in the body, as well as being acidic.

You need fats in your diet to live a healthy life. Your body uses fat to provide energy. The cells in your body are made out of a fatty cell membrane. Essential fatty acids linolenic and linoleic acid are used by the body to make omega-3 and omega-6 fatty acids, which are important in the normal functioning of all the tissues of the body. These fats are used for proper functioning of nerves and brain cells, which contain large amounts of essential fats. All our body cells contain some fats as essential parts of cell membranes, controlling what goes in and out of the cells.

Fats transport fat-soluble vitamins A, D, E, and K through the bloodstream to where they are needed. Fats also form steroid hormones, which are needed to regulate many bodily processes.[22]

The confusion with regard to fats has been due to the type of fats that we eat. Some trans fats are just plain bad for you and your liver, which has the job of trying to process them. Your liver is responsible for your metabolism and hence your ability to maintain a healthy weight. Even good oils such as olive oil and coconut oil, when heated at high temperatures, become hard for the liver to digest.

To combat this imbalance, it is necessary to eat a low-fat diet with minimal processed foods and with naturally occurring omega-3 fatty acids. The lower omega 6 to omega 3 fatty acid ratio is desirable for reducing the risk of many chronic diseases, such as heart disease, cancer, inflammation, and autoimmune diseases. Ideally, the ratio of omega-6 to omega-3 fatty acids should be between 1:1 and 4:1.[8] For this reason, try to incorporate a higher percentage of omega-3 fatty acids than omega-6 fatty acids. Some foods with omega-3 fatty acids are mackerel, salmon, sardines, flax seeds, chia seeds, and walnuts.[23]

On Carbohydrates

Carbohydrates are basically complex sugars that are broken down by the body to simple sugars such as glucose. These sugars are then pushed into our cells by the hormone insulin, produced by the pancreas. The sugars are either used for energy or stored as glycogen. The insulin is also responsible for the storage of fat. Hence the more sugars and carbohydrates you consume, the more insulin you produce to push into the cells, and the more fat you can store with the increased insulin production.

Simply put, the more carbs you eat, the more fat you will be able to store. Being overweight is a risk factor for many diseases. It would seem like a good idea to minimize the amount of insulin the body needs to produce. Also, when too much insulin is produced over time, the person can become insulin resistant and eventually diabetic.

The idea is to eat carbohydrates that minimize a strong insulin response. The general philosophy is that the more complex the carbohydrates are, the lower the glycemic index (GI) and the less insulin that is produced due to large blood sugar fluctuations.

Good fat and fiber slow down the insulin response, and so when they are eaten at the same meal, there is not as large a spike in the insulin production. This is good to keep in mind if you plan on indulging in high-carbohydrate treats.[24]

Chapter 9

TRUSTING IN LIFE

How are you traveling through life? Do you have a sense of trust that all will work out for you? Or is there an undercurrent of fear?

There are all sorts of possibilities when it comes to conscious and subconscious fear: fear of not accomplishing, fear of not getting to your appointments in time, fear that you will be rejected by people for some unknown reason, fear of those around you. There is an endless list that has been presented to you by society and the news media, not to mention your own mind. Let us look at what makes up your world and how it functions on a level other than the physical.

What Makes Your World Go Round?

By this, I mean what keeps you going? What makes your world go around smoothly? In this chapter, I will view the following points with an eye to how they affect the smooth running of your personal world. The smoother your world is, the smoother the world of those around you. Just as negativity in your environment can bring you down, being positive can help others shift to a more constructive approach to life.

I will focus on the following factors that create and affect your world on a daily basis. These are some of the things that shape your trust in life and how you live your life.

1) Your beliefs and their creations
2) The trust we have on the human plane
3) Faith in a power greater than ourselves

4) The release of fear (conscious and subconscious) in our daily lives

5) Assessing our lives in the moment

6) Humor

7) Gratitude

• **Our Beliefs and Their Creations**

Beliefs can be positive or negative, depending on how you use them to accomplish joy and satisfaction and to create relationships. Oftentimes, many of your beliefs are not really yours; they come from your family, friends, and society. Trying to change them can be a long road. You may not even know what they are because you are so used to the idea of them. You may have a goal in mind—for example, better relationships at home or work. Your beliefs would play a part seen and unseen in these relationships. Focusing on finding and changing your beliefs can lead you down a path that takes much effort and may even distract you from your goals.

When you are clear on your goals, the situation becomes simpler. You simply *declare* what you want. At first it may feel strange (or right). Each time you come up against a negative belief or speech pattern associated with your goal, remember your declaration. Declare it to yourself again with true commitment. You can say it silently and also aloud. After a while, the speech patterns and behaviors tend to disappear. If they do appear, they are associated more and more with your positive declaration. This in turn negates undesirable patterns until they do in fact disappear.

A declaration could be:

"I am comfortable around people."

"I have enough time to do all the things that I need to do."

"Everything is working out in the time scale for the good of all."

More specific declarations could be:

"Mary and I have a happy, constructive relationship."

"Joe respects my opinion."

"I eat and drink only what my body needs."

When you start out with the declarations, they may not seem real, but keep doing them, and they will take on a life of their own. They will become real. In a sense, it is another form of manifesting. You create what you focus on. Hence it is good to focus on what you truly want, not on what you fear will happen. For this reason, it is very important to be clear and declare our wants.

It is a way of avoiding being swept away with the breeze of fears and what could be. There are many belief systems surrounding you, and it is important not to lose sight of your own desires and goals in the midst of a sea of belief systems. You are responsible for your own body and soul. You are the driver of your future. The saying "No one can die for you" comes to mind. Similarly, no one else can live for you. We are all individuals with our own pathways to heaven.

• Faith and Trust in the Human Plane

Trust in yourself is a very basic need to function smoothly. You need a sense of physical trust in your body. You trust that you will wake up in the morning. You trust that your body will digest the food you eat and utilize the air you breathe. You trust that your body will heal itself, rebuild cells that are old, and replace them with new ones. For stability, you need a certain amount of trust in your friends and family.

The workplace is also where you trust. You trust that you get paid in accordance with your work. Your coworkers will work with you in a constructive way to obtain the results that are part of the job description. Others will do their jobs, providing you with transport for the food chain, electronics, and goods that you use daily.

When you cannot put faith in your coworkers, family, or body, faith in a power greater than yourself comes in to play, which is something I will talk about in the next section.

On the larger scale, you trust that nature will be there for you, and that your planet will continue to function in a way that supports your life. You trust that the sun will come up, or at least it will be a new day. That night will fall. The seasons will change, and the grass will grow. Nature spirits with farmers will produce food for the human population. The earth will continue to provide sources of energy for your use and comfort.

All these forms of trust are important to varying degrees for a stable life.

When your trust in these things fails due to fires, earthquakes, and tornados, your faith in a greater power helps to bridge the vacuum of trust, as I will be discussing in the next section.

These forms of trust are assumed for most of your life. At some point you become sick, and trust in your body is questioned. You will die, and likely it will be of an illness. Most societies have developed to the point that violence and accidents are less likely to cause death. When you have a spiritual connection to the whole and source of all, the fear associated with leaving the physical plane is reduced. There is trust that you will continue on as spirit to another reality. The sadness of leaving loved ones is the hardest part of passing to another plane.

• **Faith in a Power Greater Than Yourself**

Faith in a loving power greater than yourself takes your life from stable to a higher level of trust. It's not only in the arena of passing, but in the daily activities of your life. You can let go of some of the details in life, knowing that things will work out as needed. At the parts where trust fails you (e.g., work friends), faith can carry you, knowing that you are looked after on many levels. You can have faith that you can see the road to take, which is being shown to you. You have faith that what you want is what you need, and that what you get is what you need.

Our trust is often manifested in the form of intuition. It is an amazing time in life to live. There are so many things to see and do. There are so many choices for people to make, and there's so little time to do it in. Time is speeding up and challenging us to have faith in ourselves and our intuition. How else can we make choices to which we will never know all the background and outcomes? In a job interview, the first thirty seconds[25] decides whether or not you will get the job. I can see this. People know at some level about the other person instinctively, and they also do not have a lot of time to mull over the interview because others are waiting to be interviewed.

There was also an interesting article that stated the higher up in an organization a person was, the more the person used intuition. The rationale was that they had many decisions to make and could not have all the available information or time to find the information before the decision had to be made.

It is important for the smooth running of your life that you trust yourself and have faith in your guidance. Ultimately, it is what will carry you through difficult times.

• **Release of Fear**

The release of conscious or subconscious fear is a liberating experience. It is hard not to go through life without some sort of fear raising its head. In a way, it is easier to deal with if it is a conscious fear with a reason that is understandable and acceptable. It is harder to deal with a fear when it is subconscious. It is like a fish swimming in water, or us breathing air: it is just there, and so it's not seen or acknowledged. The news media promotes many forms of fear one disaster after another, repeated till the scenes are embedded in the subconscious. In one sense, there seems to be a fascination with disaster viewed from a distance. Possibly it is the "better them than me" syndrome. Or it could be that it helps people to value their own lives—the realization that they are in fact finite, and they could be worse off.

The only problem with this is that the fear created affects the people watching subconsciously. The subconscious is always looking to protect us. In doing so, it incorporates the messages of fear and potentially dangerous events. These events tend to get blown out of proportion, both in society and in the subconscious. I lived in Chile for years. It was a bit baffling for me to see how some people feared the country and the water simply because it was in South America. Bad press for the continent lingered, coloring the present and all the countries in South America. I felt safe traveling in Chile alone, and I thought the water where we lived was excellent. As with any country in the world, obviously dubious areas are not recommended, and accidents can happen anywhere.

Fear robs us of joy, love, peace, and confidence. In effect, it takes away all the things that make life worth living. Ignoring it is not an option that works successfully. How can we release fear?

First, you need to confront your fear, see how real the fear is, and understand where it's coming from. See if it's based on a misconception or a clear and present threat. If the fear is valid, it is important to deal with the physical situation. Remove yourself from a dangerous situation, or handle the situation in a way that is safe for you.

If the fear is something that you know you are creating internally, then it needs to be dealt with internally. Here, I am not talking about a real and present danger that we need to fear and take evasive action in order to avoid physical or emotional danger.

The most effective way to defocus internal fear is to do something that is the opposite of fear. This requires intention. Your intention can be used to release the fear. We have all used these methods or some of them, and we've done it instinctively at times. Now, I am talking about using them with intention when we feel fear. The combination of intention and defocusing the fear creates a shift in your being. The following are some examples of defocusing fear.

- Look at or talk to someone you love.
- Do something that gives you joy.
- Think of a peaceful scene.
- Use your breath. Breathe in white light or the color that comes to you. Breathe slowly through your solar plexus.
- Do a simple standing or sitting exercise, breathing in and out.
- Remember a time when you were confident
- Feel gratitude for the things around you—even an ant crawling determinedly on its path to the collective hole.
- Remember that the next moment will be different from this one. Each moment changes your feelings and perspective. Decide that the next moments will be full of confidence and faith in the future. Know that you are protected and safe.
- In the case of fear of performing when you are overwhelmed and frightened by what you need to do that day, think of what you have done so far for a few minutes. Make a

mental list—it will surprise you. Do not judge the activities; because you did them, they are worthy. Then you can go on to do things associated with your next goal. In this way, you release some of the performance fear.

- Last but not least, be patient with yourself. Give yourself the same consideration you would a beloved pet.

What all these techniques have in common is that you are going to go where fear is not. It is like looking at the complimentary color or choosing another door to enter.

You cannot be in different *places* at once. In other words, while doing something in one emotion, you cannot have another emotion. Shifting to another space, if only for seconds, changes the dynamics of fear.

• **Our Lives in the Moment**

I have talked about living in the moment in chapter 6, but I will cover it briefly here in a light aligned with trusting in life.

Each moment creates your life. What you focus on for that moment is creating your life for the moment and the future. With that in mind, ignore the small irritations, such as harsh words or flies buzzing around your head. Be kind to yourself. Be patient. Rome was not built in a day. The lessons you are learning are over a lifetime. Sometimes you cannot know what the effects of the moment are into the future. It may seem like a bad moment, but one never knows.

A friend who loves gardening and grows her own vegetables confided in me that she was bored by the routine tasks. It was a surprise to me because from my viewpoint, I considered her lucky to be in that situation. It was a reminder for me that, yes, simply doing things to get them done or have a result is repetitive and boring in the end.

On the other hand, talking to Gaia, the earth mother, as you work changes things. Talking to the plants and enjoying and encouraging them also changes things. Living in the moment with an awareness greater than yourself and the mundane task at hand brings you, the plants, and the earth into another plane of awareness. This awareness is spread through the network of Gaia energy to the earth. The end result is not boring or repetitive, because each moment is different in the same way that each cloud is different. Each snowflake is different. Each person is different. Each moment is different.

• Humor

We often take ourselves so seriously that we miss out on our lives. We miss the details of appreciation. Without humor, life becomes a chore. We find it harder to connect with spirit.

Babies are said to laugh three hundred times[26] a day, whereas adults laugh only fifteen to twenty times a day. I imagine that increasing this number even by a couple of laughs would make a huge difference to your life and health. It is easier to let go of stress when you see the bright side. It also means you are not in a space of fear or stress. You are in a space to enjoy what life has to offer.

I will never forget an Australian politician who was on after the news one night. He was happily sitting at a desk and reading out hate mail that had been sent to him. He really seemed to think it was very funny, and he was laughing at some of it. It was hard not to laugh with him. This was something I had never expected a politician to do. He certainly did not appear to be taking himself or his hate mail too seriously.

However, I encourage you to forget the news and TV. Think of your own personal movie. Rerun the scenes. Do you want to add more comedy, or more awe, or more accomplishment? Remember a friend you always share a laugh with and note how it feels. Looking back on it, often there was not a real joke, simply a sense of fun and finding joy and amusement in the idiosyncrasies of life. Ask yourself while you are waiting in line, "What are the most significant, fun, humorous moments in my life?"

• **Forgiveness**

I have mentioned the importance of forgiveness several times throughout this book. Forgiveness shifts our relationship with other people and ourselves for the better, and sometimes in dramatic ways. There are several areas where forgiveness comes into play.

You have most probably heard of karma before. Usually it's used in reference to past lives or even this life. The idea of karma is what goes around comes around. In other words, you pay for your transgressions in your next life or reincarnation, which is determined by your actions in this life. We may also come into karmic relationships without knowing about it. I believe that this is often the case—the unknown person who would not let your permit pass, or the friend who has it in for you for no known reason. When we forgive these people and have them forgive us, there is not the same level of karmic energy connected with the relationship.

The simplest way to give and receive this forgiveness is through the

Ho'o pono pono, which I referred to in chapters 1 and 2. The Hawaiian forgiveness ceremony involves your higher spiritual levels communicating with those of the other person through divine connection. The beauty of it is that you do not even have to know what the issues were that separated you in the past. In the expanded version, you are also forgiving them and their ancestors, friends, and relatives from the beginning of time. That is quite a while, and it's quite a list. You may also have a specific event you want to forgive or be forgiven for. The important thing is to be sincere in your forgiveness. It may only take a second, but the feelings should be there with intention.

At one time, I had a friend whom I could not get along with for some reason. There was nothing concrete and no apparent argument between us. She was always very nice to me. However, I still dreaded seeing her. Then one day, on the way to meet her for lunch, I decided to do the expanded Ho'o pono pono version on her. I did it only once. The most amazing thing happened. There was absolutely no discomfort between us anymore. I was very happy to see her and have lunch with her. It was a completely different relationship. We continued to meet with the same result; the awkwardness had simply evaporated.

Then there is the everyday kind of forgiveness. You get annoyed at someone (a partner or friend) for something. This is more to do with mood and stories than karma. The Ho'o pono pono works for this too. The secret is to be in a sincere place emotionally, where you can forgive and be forgiven.

The last case is when you need to forgive yourself. You can do the

Ho'o pono pono on yourself as well. It is a good exercise and feels wonderful.

Chapter 10

JOY IN SERVING

What do I mean by serving? The simple answer is anything that you do with love and joy that supports others and the planet. I have included the caveat *with love and joy* for a reason. To help and support with resentment, reluctance, and a victim stance does not support anyone, including yourself.

Serving also involves caring for yourself. If you are not well, how can you care for others? The assumption in serving is that you are taken care of first—your spiritual, physical, emotional, and financial state. True, these states do not have to be 100 percent in order to serve. In fact, serving improves your own well-being when done with consideration for the reality of your own conditions and with a generous spirit toward others.

What does serving others really mean? Should you join the Red Cross? Save the earth? Join a charity group? All these groups and more are valuable and are important activities to contribute to yourself and the planet.

What I am talking about here is a more subtle and general form of serving. You also serve when you help someone with large parcels, when you cook a meal for others, or when you give information that someone needs from your knowledge base which they may lack. There are many ways to serve, large and small. Some people serve via their chosen carriers, others as a hobby (in the sense that they are not financially enumerated), and still others by accident and without intention.

Many years ago, I was in a hospital looking for a friend who was a medical student. For me, it was a large and confusing place. I was quite lost. I asked a passing medical student where my friend was. Instead of giving me directions, he walked me through the corridors to find him. I was a little embarrassed because I was changing his schedule. He simply smiled at me and said, "You will do the same for someone else." There was nothing I could say to that. I thought to myself, *He's right.* He was giving me a lovely example of the philosophy "What goes around comes around." I have never forgotten that kindness.

There are ways to serve that are still serving but may not have as much benefit for the person serving. You will still be helping others, but you need to be cautious of the effects it will have on you. For example, if you serve out of guilt or a craving for attention, or only because it is "the right thing to do," purely for your own advantage, or because your friends are doing it, the energy that you put into it will drain you. The outcome will not be optimum for those you are serving or yourself. That is, you can still be helping others and serving, but the benefits to yourself and others may not be as welcoming.

When you truly serve others, including the earth that supports you, you will feel invigorated and renewed. Things will fall into place for you to help you accomplish these goals. The secret of serving is to serve in a way that makes you happy. Use your talents—and we all have them—in a way that serves both you and the thing that you want to serve.

Understanding Yourself and Your Talents

Oftentimes, you are not aware of all your talents. You may underestimate yourself and be overly critical. There is pressure from society to perform in sometimes extreme ways. Television is telling you how you are to behave in an indirect and sometimes direct way. It is often sending a message of fear with negative news that is disempowering on a personal level. There are few examples of people empowered to help the society and succeeding. Society in general has assumed expectations of us. In the face of these messages, it is easy to be critical of who you are without necessarily looking for your strengths.

When you serve others, you find confidence in the positive things that you do. You also start to see other aspects of your abilities and nature that may not otherwise manifest themselves. With these experiences, you may find that you are better at some things than others. It may be a surprise to you, or it can be an already known quantity.

An example could be that you may feel strongly that some environmental changes need to be made. With this in mind, you think that you should join a group working on those changes. However, at the same time, you are extremely uncomfortable with groups. The meetings you attended made you feel that you cannot contribute in a group environment, but you want to do something. There may be activities that better suit your personality and schedule—things that you enjoy, such as research or making calls. They still allow you to serve, but within the parameters of your talents and in a way that you enjoy and feel comfortable with.

Finding your place and understanding your own needs in serving others is a very liberating and growing experience. It also adds joy to the world.

Creates Purpose in Your Life

We all crave a purpose in life, so that our lives are not just about surviving and making a living, or even just about having fun.

It is important to you and your well-being to feel as if you make a difference on some level, even if it is only making someone you care about smile. The more you feel you have a purpose in life, the more confident you become, thus enabling you to have greater strength to be yourself. The annoying things in life are just that, annoying, but they're not the focus of your life. When you have an overall focus in life, it puts the rest of your life into perspective.

What is it that you want to do with your life? You have a finite time here on earth. What do you want to remember at the end of your life, and what do you want to be remembered for? Think of a very famous movie star who made an incredible impression during her career. She was famous and well-known by all. However, twenty years down the road, most people would not even know her name. This goes for many walks of life, where people have spent their lives building fame and fortune. Time, like the water eroding a riverbed, makes us all a distant memory in the passage of years. All that we really have is the moment that we live; expecting something to be remembered is futile, with few exceptions. As the saying goes, time is the great equalizer.

So, what is it that you want to do with the time you have? Usually, people are too busy simply surviving to consider this question. There are meals to prepare and work to be done, money to earn and family and friends to meet. There's news to read and TV to watch, not to mention cleaning and showering and exercising.

A full life. So why should you help others?

You may not be recognized or remembered for you contribution. But as I pointed out earlier, in the long term, who is? What is important is that in being of service, you are fulfilling your role in life at another level.

You are contributing to the ongoing network of life in a positive way. You are expressing who you are and what you can do to contribute to the world. The butterfly effect suggests that the motion of the wings of a butterfly in Asia affect life in America.[27] This concept indicates that all is connected, and all is important. You may not be famous, but you will make a difference to yourself and others.

The way you earn money is given a new dimension when you do it with a sense of serving others. You are going beyond the mundane and reaching for the spirit of all that is. Serving others puts a positive spin on your actions, and it gives you a deeper sense of your importance and a place in the world.

This is also true of the activities you do that are not job related. In non-job-related activities, it may be easier for you to see the connection of serving others as well as the connection to those around you. When you are connected to those around you, you are also connecting to the flow of universal energy that surrounds us all.

Satisfaction in Helping Others

When you do serve with love and balance in your life, it goes without saying that you derive a great deal of satisfaction from your actions. If the goal you are involved in is large, the satisfaction will need to come from each chunk of effort that you put out. The satisfaction will need to come from the doing and not necessarily the end result. It involves confidence to know that the end goal will be met. Maybe it's not in your shift, but each piece in the puzzle makes the whole. That will be the satisfaction that you attain: being a piece of the puzzle, and knowing your talents are contributing.

When the goals are short term, like making a meal, the satisfaction will be easier to feel, even while you are cooking or preparing the meal.

If you are not feeling the satisfaction, it is a sign that you need to reassess either the task or your attitude to the task you have set yourself. Make changes until you feel a sense of satisfaction when doing the task or when it is done.

Connecting with Like-minded People

Humans in general are social animals. Even introverts need social connection. Without this social network, people feel isolated, and life becomes focused on things that may not be positive for the person involved. Loneliness, even with superficial friends present, can be a problem.

It is not always easy with the many commitments that we have between work and family to find friends that we can relate to on a deeper level. Being involved in an activity that you love, even if it is not a group activity, will bring you into contact with other people also interested in those activities or connected with them.

This gives you a head start in finding friends to whom you can relate. They are more likely to have similar beliefs and interests. Mothers with school-age children often find friends from the groups of other parents at the school and can relate to them through their children. This is a case of not being in a particular group, per se, but still meeting people with similar interests (i.e., the children), which can start the ball rolling in finding social contacts.

Using Our Natural Gifts from Spirit

When you serve others, your natural gifts are reflected back to you. You may be a good listener or a good talker, or you may be good at organizing. When you follow your intuition and do the things you like to do for others, your natural gifts become apparent. By knowing this, you can enjoy yourself and others at a higher level.

Even an introvert who is not very social will have attributes that others do not. They could communicate electronically via the vast network that is developing on earth. There would be ways to serve and help others not as gifted in this area. They could be helping a group that needs support, or family and friends who need help in this arena.

Viewing your actions as serving others will let you see by your results and enthusiasm what your gifts are.

Remove Self-talk

We are all born with, and accumulate over the years, a large amount of self-talk. Eventually it becomes something that you do not even realize you do. There is an accumulation of messages from your family and friends, as well as society. These messages may be very well meaning or not so understanding of who you are. You then interpret these messages depending on your upbringing and predisposition. The result is conversations in your head that you do not even know you are having. It's much like being held to the earth by gravity, being unaware of its pull as the earth hurdles through space.

Sometimes the silent conversations in your head surface, and you get a wow moment as you look at where your thoughts and feelings are coming from.

When you start doing things with a sense of service, it starts to override the potentially negative conversations. There is something bigger than you involved. It is a distraction from your own silent conversation.

Service also leads you to a higher plane, where such conversations are not as important. It's like being on a mountaintop: the perspective changes and makes your stories appear much smaller than they do when you are in the midst of it all.

Connect to a Greater Reality

So where does spirit fit into this? How do you connect to spirit and your soul by serving others?

The main thing to remember about serving is that it needs to be something that you enjoy. If you are not enjoying the experience, or even the satisfaction of the experience, then you are not serving at a deeper level. The energy you put forth will drain you and those around you. This will not serve spirit or your soul purpose.

Your own enjoyment in serving is paramount to success for you and those around you. Success in this case is adding positive energy to the earth. It is feeding your soul and your spirit. There may be many karmic connections that you are fulfilling without realizing it. There may be many spiritual lessons that you are learning in the guise of serving.

If you do not enjoy serving, stop and look at why. Is it not a good fit due to time, group philosophy, subject matter, or personality?

There are many ways to be of service. Cooking a meal is of service to the family—but again, not when it is cooked with resentment and stress. When you are not appreciated by those around you, it may give you a clue as to your approach to the task. When you cook with love and service, it comes through in the food and the approach. Being in a time crunch may change the way you cook. Ask for help, do less cooking, or make simpler meals, and enjoy it more. In the end, both you and your family will notice and appreciate the difference. Initially the changes may require patience for everyone, as all changes do, however when the goal is to serve, that will also come through in the end. Your food takes on a spiritual energy prepared with love and care.

How do you find this joy in serving? By focusing on yourself and being connected with yourself. In this way, you will be focused and connected with all. How can you focus on yourself to find joy? Move slowly, breathe deeply and focus on your body. Another way is to take a few seconds to focus on an object in detail. See the beauty in it, even if it is only a cup: note the material it is made out of, the color, the shape. This transports you to another framework and takes you out of your mind and patterns for a short time. Only seconds can make a difference in balancing your mood and emotions.

I used this technique in a particularly stressful time of my life. Often I was fortunate enough to have a piece of nature visible, and I would focus on that piece whenever I became overwhelmed.

It was only for seconds, but it changed my approach to the whole situation that had caused me stress. It could see the benefits of what appeared to be negative. We need to defocus in ordered to focus clearly.

We tend to think that we are isolated beings. Aside from your work, friends, and family, you do not usually consider your actions to have an effect on those around you, and vice versa. The spiritual reality of the world, on the other hand, is that we are all connected.

It is easy to avoid doing a small task of service when no one would know you had missed the opportunity, and you feel that you are not responsible for the task. An example of this comes to mind. One morning when I was jogging, I noticed about fifty sharp nails that had been dropped in an intersection. It was halfway through my jog. Nobody was around on that side of the road. I was not using a car, and so obviously I would not suffer when the nails penetrated a tire. I thought to myself, *Well, maybe they will not go through a tire. Somebody else will clean them up. That is what the city workers do.* But then I looked at all those nails shining in the sunlight, and I started to pick them up. In the meantime, other people had appeared, both on foot and in cars. I supposed that I looked foolish. I even had the thought that people may think that I was dropping them. I put them all in my fanny pack and continued jogging with the heavier load. I gave them to the hotel I was staying at to use, because they were nice, big new nails.

The point of this story is even though I was not responsible for the nails, and no one would really know of my good deed, it still felt good to do something for other people. I imagined even one car with a nail in the tire, and the driver not knowing where he got it and having to fix the leak. It was something I would not want for myself, and hence it was not something I would want for others.

We are all connected, whether or not we know it. Each action we take affects others. We are all connected spiritually, but we are also all connected physically. There is a chain reaction.

When you do something of service, large or small, you are adding to the spirit and the reality of this planet. The ripples go unseen and seen through the networks connecting us to all that is in our universe. It is impossible for you to be alone; if you think you are, it is an illusion.

Chapter 11

A LIFE THAT SHINES

Paying attention to spirit shows you another dimension of reality. It makes your life shine.

The awareness of an aura about an object expands to become an aura about you and hence causes a shift in the vision of your life. There is a glow that is added to your life. This glow makes everything shine: your health, your relationships, your work, and your play. Whenever you look anywhere and see the beauty of spirit, your life is enriched.

The advantages of seeing the spiritual in the ordinary physical existence are as follows.

We expand our physical world to include something magical.

Yes, spirit is something that is not defined and is not as visible as the physical world. This is in a sense what makes it magical. We have to shift our focus away from the everyday viewpoints to see the magic around us. This defocusing also gives us more perspective in our everyday lives.

Just as taking a short break when working on a project gives you new ideas on the project, many great discoveries have their starting point when people are taking a shower or are relaxed, letting in the messages from spirit. Similarly, when you first wake up in the morning and are not really yet in the physical reality of the day, you find that ideas flow.

These connections and ideas from spirit can save a lot of time and energy in the physical world. Ideas come to you, bringing clarity and focus to a task that may have been confusing or tedious.

Agreement with the world around you reduces your stress levels and can add a new, enjoyable element to your life.

Start making agreements with things as well as people around you. When you do this, you add another dimension to your daily life. It can become a game. You can test your magic muscle. Make it playful, not another competition or task that needs to be done. Bring some fun into your life. Then be grateful for the magic that flows from it. You can actually start seeing the results of spirit in all things, as well as your connection with it.

It can be something as simple as asking a lock to open easily. It could be guessing the time without a watch. Maybe you can see an aura about an object by defocusing and looking at the object in a relaxed way.

Experiment with a pendulum for questions you may have. See what you come up with yourself to incorporate spirit into your daily life.

It adds an element of fun to your life.

Exercises and experiments enable your body and mind to incorporate the knowledge of the physical plane with spiritual energy. Do these experiments with fun and avoid judging yourself. There is no failing in this arena. It is an exercise in connecting with spirit; there can be no failure in that. The fact you are making an effort will connect you in some form with spirit, expanding your world.

It incorporates a new version of your reality—an upgrade, if you will.

With practice, you open yourself up to a spiritual reality bit by bit. Each time you connect with spirit and acknowledge it in your daily life, you are shifting your reality.

You become more adept at manifesting on a regular basis.

Being clear that you are connected to spirit in your daily life helps you to have confidence in your ability to manifest as well. You have seen the bigger picture of spirit in your life, and so you are clear that what you want to manifest can appear.

Dealing with the challenges of life becomes easier, and you become more confident.

You are opening yourself up to learning and communicating on many different levels. Your portfolio of life has taken a leap that enables you to deal with the challenges of life in a more confident light. It enables you to see the blessings that you have in a way that supports your life.

You can more easily see the beauty within yourself and others.

This is a wonderful piece of magic. So often you are shown or see the negative with regard to yourself and others. Life appears to be all about striving for something and not ever getting there. There is no time to smell the roses and see the beauty. When you see the spirit in the world you inhabit, you have a deeper understanding of how much of a masterpiece you and all things around you truly are. The beauty of the moment can take your breath away. The beauty surrounding you becomes evident. Recognizing the beauty that you are as a physical manifestation of spirit becomes the norm.

It helps you in the process of attaining unconditional love for yourself and others.

Unconditional love relieves you of many stories in your head that are connected to your belief systems. Unconditional love is a natural consequence when relating to spirit. Spirit does not judge us as we judge ourselves. The more you connect with spirit, the greater your ability to unconditionally love yourself and others.

It improves the society in which you live.

Your own development increases the development of the greater good in society. We are all connected by spirit. As a consequence, when you develop, so does society. You may choose to help this along physically by taking a greater interest in the community around you in some form. Or you may simply develop your own connection to spirit, which will then be transmitted to society as a whole. Remember, every single soul counts!

All these advantages are a process, which we as individuals and as a society are developing. Some societies are more focused than others in this development, as are some individuals. The earth is like a large school, and rates of development will differ; that is perfect for the total development. Each soul is learning. Each soul has been permitted to enroll in the school.

Level of Confidence

Spiritual reality increases your level of confidence, both in yourself and in society as a whole.

On a personal level, you start to realize that you are supported in ways you cannot consciously fathom at this point in time. You start to see signs of this support. It can be in the form of oracle cards mentioned in chapter 3; you select them, and they have a very personal meaning and significance to you. One time the first card on the bottom of the deck resonated with me, but I decided that I should have shuffled the deck first. My feeling was that if it was in fact the message I needed at that time, I would get it again. I shuffled the deck well and picked the same card again from the middle of the deck. This has happened on a consistent basis, to the point I am confident that the card I pick is the correct message and the right support for me at the time.

This increases your self-confidence. You know when you start listening to spirit and your soul, you will do what is correct for you and hence what is correct for those around you. It also increases the level of patience you have, both for yourself and those around you.

You are guided by your spirit to know that others have soul purposes they are fulfilling. They may not be as clear about it or interact with spirit in the same way, but they too have a mission. It is not for us to judge their level of participation or awareness of their souls' purpose. It becomes easier to have patience when you realize this.

You know also that things will work out for the best. You know how to manifest and allow the appropriate time for all to create the manifestation. You are clear that events are for the good of all. Even events that seemed traumatic and undesirable at the time shift to be beneficial for your life and those around you.

You realize you do not have all the information, and hence there is a degree of trust, and then positive experience, that reinforces this attitude. Reinforcing your thought processes with positive affirmations is an excellent support for when you are feeling off color.

When you realize that you are part of all, and that everything that you think and do makes a difference on a physical as well as nonphysical level, it changes you. You have more strength and interest in focusing on issues for the good of all. When you know that you personally are supported by spirit, it makes actions and thoughts that were difficult become much clearer and easier to accomplish.

Why, Oh Why?

Life becomes dull when we do things in an automatic fashion, when we do not connect with our soul and intuition. We look for more and more stimuli, which can lead to depression, addictions, and generally a dull life.

The reasonable question then arises: "What am I doing in my job, or with my friends, or in my life in general?" However, I think the way it is asked is usually negative, without the expectation of an answer. The answers, if they do come, are often depressing. "I have to make a living. I have no choice. They will be offended if I do not go."

I believe that part of the reason life can be dull is that we have many layers of fear and resentment covering our minds and souls.

When you are living in a spiritual reality, or a reality that includes spirit, you can ask the same question and receive an answer. For example, if your instincts are telling you to apply for the job you happen to see in the paper, you do so knowing that it will lead you to something connected with your job search. If it's not the job you want, maybe it's a person or a job that is recommend to you.

If you have an uncomfortable feeling about a person you are thinking of forming a deeper relationship with, and you are not sure why, ask spirit, "Is this relationship for the highest and best for me at this time?" in reference to the potential relationship. Then let the question go with the intention that in the next twenty-four or forty-eight hours, you will receive a clear insight into your question.

You can also ask spirit whether you should attend a specific function on a specific day. If the answer you get in your gut feeling is yes, but you are still hesitant about going, you can ask why it is recommended that you go. Is it for the food, or to meet some interesting people who can help you in some way? Perhaps it is for pleasant company, or simply to treat yourself to a reward.

Whatever answer resonates with you is the correct answer. Then you have something to look forward to without confusion or guilt. You connect with spirit and realize that this is something positive and beneficial for you. It becomes something that cannot turn into a bad experience, because you have the confidence to know you are doing the right thing. You can relax and enjoy the experience.

I was guided to go to a social gathering of my chiropractor, where I knew no one. I did not argue with my guidance because over the years, I have learned it is very beneficial. I ended up meeting someone there who has been a close friend for decades. In retrospect, it was worthwhile to go.

There are many ways of connecting with your guides. As I mentioned earlier, there is kinesiology muscle testing, which chiropractors use to test for recommended vitamins and muscle imbalances. The body can act as an amazing tool that can provide us with feedback. Self-muscle testing allows us to connect with the inner spirit and bypass our conscious processing.

There are any number of questions you can ask when using self-muscle testing or kinesiology testing, which has been used as a diagnostic health tool by chiropractors. The technique I mentioned in the preface accurately accesses the electric system and can be used any time we need to address a physical, emotional, mental, or soul-level problem by reading the strength or weakness of our muscles. Self-muscle testing involves using the fingers on your hand for a yes/no response.

Some questions you can ask are:

- When or where are recommended events to attend?
- Which particular emotions need to be resolved or diffused?
- Is a certain food causing me problems?

- Which supplements to take, A or B or C, and how many per day?
- Which option is better, A or B?

Muscle testing accesses your intuitive and energetic systems. It is not a replacement for conventional medical diagnostics. Do not rely on muscle testing alone to determine whether you have an illness, food sensitivity, or other serious condition.

I have used kinesiology with practice for shopping (which I am not fond of), and for deciding when and where I need to go. It is a way of connecting with your spirit, higher self, and guides. The way you ask the questions for the yes/ no response is very important. It is a very literal method of receiving a response. Another way of doing this is with a pendulum or dousing rod. There are many ways of connecting with spirit on a physical response level. As a scientist, I love the yes/no response.

I have had wonderful success and many experiences to verify that I am in fact connected to a higher power and knowledge base. I have used it to decide when is a good time to go on holidays. The results have always been impressive. One holiday was more dramatic than usual. In 2011, I went to Ireland and Scotland for the first time. Travelling off season and avoiding the crowds, even though the weather may be dubious, is my preferred time to vacation. I spent a month traveling as far as the Orkney Islands, where I stayed for two weeks. It was a wonderful holiday. The stories of rain did not eventuate, not even in the Orkney Islands, the islands farthest north in Scotland. In the one month there, there was one day of rain. Everything had been booked two months in advance.

At the time, the volcano in Iceland was disrupting many flights. I was told by friends that I would not get there due to fight cancelations. I *knew* through guidance that I would. I flew into Dublin in the morning. The day before, the planes did not fly. As

I was going into the city in Dublin, the shuttle driver said it was the last plane to land, and they were closing the airports. I had made it into Dublin in a half-day window! For me, that also meant even fewer people in the hotels. By the time my holiday was over, Dublin was crowded with tourists again.

The connection with spirit and my guidance certainly made my life shine!

The trick is to listen to the instinct that is calling to you. This is another form of asking spirit to help on a daily basis. Whether you call it intuition or use methods of dousing, it helps you to pay attention to what you want in your life and what is important. It also guides you to listen in a nonattached way. I should mention again that with any form of self-muscle testing, if you are attached, you can lean the results in the direction of your attachment and so invalidate the result. For muscle testing, you also need to be well hydrated and formulate the questions clearly.

Removing Confusion to Reveal the Shine to Life

In this case, I am defining *confusion* as being derived from our belief systems. Our belief systems basically determine what we do in life and how we do it. They can be conscious or subconscious belief systems. Either way, they work to determine or actions. So, what about these belief systems can cause a lack of shine in our lives?

1) The most obvious one is life is hard or unfair, or the good loose and the powerful win. Each one of these could be a long topic of discussion. However, I think you realize that most people believe these sayings to differing degrees. When you recognize these as negative belief systems and not the truth of reality, you shift the possibilities into the positive realm.

2) The general belief in most societies is that success is based on accumulated financial gains. Some societies and individuals are less influenced by this belief. Traditionally, less technological societies believe more in the knowledge base of people, such as their wisdom or heritage. This would still likely gain them more material advantages over the population. In technological societies accumulation of goods or luxurious living quarters has become a top priority. The size of houses is getting larger and larger, and conversely the size of yards are getting smaller. Technology has made life move so rapidly that the spiritual aspects of our society are lost in the rush for more and better, not survival. The desire for the end result has overcome the joy of traveling on the path to get there. Of course, once there, it is a short moment to the next goal, a short moment to shine for your goals, and even a short time for your life to shine.

3) Another dulling agent in our lives is the belief that we need to be serious in order to be taken seriously and considered successful. There is also the belief that work is not fun. If it is fun, it is not work and it does not count. These beliefs can be combined into an even more subtle one.

   This belief says that the more work you have and the more serious you are, and the more stressed you are, the more important you are.

   It works for any level of society and job description. Each country and individual will have a differing degree of these belief systems, and it will affect the shine level of their population accordingly. In a technological, puritan-based society like the United States, it can be quite strong, as reflected in the short holidays and dedication to work. Europeans are often more balanced with more holidays to enjoy their lives away from work. This balance relives and shifts the intensity of the time that they are at work. I am not saying that taking more holidays is the answer to creating a shining life. It is simply one of the indicators that something other than work, and the strong belief system in it, is less valued in some countries.

These are all things to be aware of. The more you try to fight them, the more ingrained they are. I mention them as things to observe and release. The more you focus on them, the more real they become. Instead, shift your focus to connect with spirit in some form to bring back balance into your belief system. You could even substitute the word *work* for *play* or something that connects you with joy.

Everything You Do Is Part of Spirit

Everything that exists is here because we are part of spirit. When your spirit leaves your body, you die. When your body dies, your spirit leaves; the spark of life is gone. The spark of your spirit keeping you here has gone.

We are holding this world together with our belief, energy, and manifestations. When we no longer put energy into the world, it is like a flower wilting without water, and an ocean without waves that has grown stagnant. The world starts to erode. It's much like your body starts to erode when you do not nurture it. How do you feed the force that feeds us?

How do you feed spirit? You nurture spirit when you can see beyond the physical to the spirit within. You can visualize the atoms that compose the material world, and in the magic of their spinning, you see that you also are magical.

You can also incorporate spirit in your physical activities. Whatever activity you are involved in can be shifted to a cause greater than yourself. It could be a broad cause (for the good of all, for the safety of the whales, for honor in politics) or a narrow cause (for my brother's son, supporting my ill friend). It's something that calls to you that you want to support.

Each time you do this with intention, it will give energy to your declared cause. It is like a physical donation of sorts. The energy is transmitted to your declared cause through the connection of all that is. Benefits to you are a greater depth of empowerment in whatever you do. The connection with spirit and realization of an energy beyond the physical will become real and clear in a level of deeper perception. It also makes the activity in the physical plane easier.

You need to balance between heaven and earth, the physical and the spiritual. You obtain your sustenance from the earth. It is important to remember that. The grounding from the earth helps you balance your physical and spiritual natures. An exercise in grounding is to sit quietly with your feet flat on the ground. Do it inside or outside, with or without shoes. Imagine that you have etheric roots that are spreading deeply into the earth. As you exhale, imagine the roots getting deeper. As you inhale, draw up loving energy from the earth. Walking barefooted on the earth or sand for ten minutes is also a good way to ground your energy.

Chapter 12

TRANSFORM INTO THE LIGHT

You are the light!

The only transformation that occurs is the shift in viewpoint of yourself and the reality around you. Do not fear; you cannot get it wrong. Whatever you do with intention for the good of all will shift you as a being in a way that is beneficial for all. This is a given because this is what you have intended. At times, you may feel it is not enough or you are not enough. When this happens, breathe deeply and ask for spirit to guide and support you in a direction that includes the greater picture of spirit in your physical reality. This shifts your focus to release the fears (conscious and subconscious) that may be surrounding you.

Each of us is a torch in the darkness. Let your light shine!

Light shows you the way! It is something that lights your way. You are that light.

How do you let your light shine? You be who you are in full color. You incorporate and embrace your physical as well as your spiritual self. Together, you are a powerhouse. Your fears of being you are transformed into being you in alignment with the spiritual plane that you are part of and serving. You accept yourself for the wonderful being that you are, and for your part in all that is. You have the courage to express yourself on this plane.

In this way, you add light to others. We are all connected on the spiritual plane as well as the physical plane. Likely you will not know how or why you have affected others. With the connection to spirit, the effect you have on others will be for the good of all. This is a wonderful feeling and gives you confidence you can let your light shine in full color. When you are the true you, you become an inspiration to others. It's not important whether or not you know consciously what that effect is.

As I write, there is an incredible lady upstairs. She is seventy-nine years old and is as agile as a sixty-year-old. Yes, she has wrinkles, but she looks about ten years younger. She has lived a full life, retiring only four years ago. The magical thing about her is her smile. She has the most incredible smile full of humor, patience, understanding, and love. She is a wonder to be around. I know she has her share of earthly concerns, however she seems to be operating on a different plane. She is a shining light to all those who come into contact with her.

We wander through life thinking we have limited powers—the powers that are connected with physical reality. Do not get me wrong: these physical powers are very useful and enjoyable as well. Walking, eating, talking, caring, planning, and working in the physical plane are great activities. However, we were created for so much more. Our souls are calling out for more. Your skin is regenerated in twenty-seven days.[28] Scientifically, our bodies are supposed to live for 120 years.[29] So why do so many people age earlier? Why are they turning down their lights?

I believe people have their reasons for being here, and they have their lessons to learn on this plane right now. So, yes, many may choose to leave this plane at an earlier time. Others may accept sickness as a natural part of life rather than delve into preventive medicine or delve into alternate views of our human nature; they may also have lessons to learn from the process. These are choices we have the freedom to make.

There are also those who want to change their lives but are not quite sure how. They feel something is missing in their lives, but they are not sure what, and the missing factor is likely not on the nightly news. As I have talked about in this book, I feel the missing factor is relating to spirit on a daily basis. This gives meaning to each moment and day, beyond the physical activities you carry out. In fact, it transforms these activities. When you connect with your internal spirit, you recognize your power and can take control of your life, shifting yourself toward the light.

How do you become more of your complete self?

- Look to your inner guidance for what you can do and cannot do. The guidance will take into account what is good for you as a soul, as well as what soul purpose you wanted to fulfill in your journey here.
- Release the fear that holds you. The fear is usually based on beliefs that you should be a certain way and do a certain thing. These beliefs do not hold true for who you really are.
- Operate from a picture larger than yourself. This enables you to see your place in the world and also in the goals of spirit for this plane.
- Do what you enjoy and gives you satisfaction. Often this is what your soul needs. The joy and the commitment shift your view of the world to one of contentment, a knowing that you are on the path you need to travel at this time. It's the type of work that makes your heart sing. It's a hobby that gives joy to your life. It's supporting those in need or sharing love and joy with family and friends.
- Find yourself in awe of something greater than yourself every day. It could be music, nature, dancing, or a sporting event—something that, for you, reveals the spiritual in the mundane. It's something that brings you joy and allows you to express who you truly are.

When you are grateful, you automatically shine. When you are grateful, you are giving thanks for the things and people around you. You are thanking spirit for these creations. You are thanking and acknowledging the physical creations for their spiritual source.

The easiest way to shine is to be grateful. This connects you with spirit.

∞ **Summary** ∞

Uniting Your Spiritual and Physical Self: Transforming the Ordinary into the Extraordinary

- Everything is by agreement, including our relationship with inanimate objects.
- Learning is the goal; there is no good or bad, only consequences from which we learn.
- Being grateful is the easiest way to remove the boundaries between earth and spirit.
- Unconditional love connects us to spirit and makes the world go around. Forgiveness comes naturally.
- Living moment by moment connects you with spirit in the moment, uniting spirit with physical reality.
- Including spirit in physical reality gives you a level of confidence that makes your life shine.
- Everything and everyone surrounding us is a gift.
- Live a longer, healthier life connecting with spirit.
- Travel through life with trust and faith.
- Connect to spirit by serving others.
- Let your light shine.
- You are transforming into the light.

About the Author

With her unique background and spiritual guidance, Lydia is focused on helping others to combine the spiritual and physical realities of life.

Lydia's scientific studies into the microscopic physical world give her a unique understanding of the subtle energies unseen by the human eye. After obtaining her doctorate in chemistry at Carnegie-Mellon University, Pittsburgh, Lydia worked in research in the education and corporate worlds. She carried out experiments based on electromagnetic principles to determine the structure of compounds on a molecular level.

Giving consulting and training courses in Feng Shui shifted her focus to the spiritual arena. She consults for business and residential Feng Shui clients in the United States, Spain, Ireland, and South America. Lydia currently lives with her husband in the Patagonia region of Chile.

She can be contacted through her website at www.LydiaMitchell.com.

Upcoming Books

9 Ways to Relax into a Magic Life: The Secrets
    of Treading Lightly
Contentment Now
Connecting to the Source: A Simple Manual
Seeing the Beauty Within: A Freedom to Be

Endnotes

1   "Although the term *monism* is derived from Western philosophy to typify positions in the mind–body problem, it has also been used to typify religious traditions. In the general definition a philosophy is monistic if it postulates unity of origin of all things." Source: Wikipedia.

2   " Omnism is the recognition and respect of all religions; those who hold this belief are called omnists (or Omnists). The Oxford English Dictionary (OED) quotes as the term's earliest usage by English poet Philip J. Bailey in 1839: 'I am an omnist, and believe in all religions.' Many omnists say that all religions contain truths, but that no one religion offers all that is truth." Source: Wikipedia.

3   Linear illusion of time: Eternalism (philosophy of time). "Eternalism is a philosophical approach to the ontological nature of time, which takes the view that all points in time are equally *real*, as opposed to the presentism idea that only the present is real. Eternalism is the view that each spacetime moment exists in and of itself. Modern advocates often take inspiration from the way time is modeled as a dimension in the theory of relativity, giving time a similar ontology to that of space (although the basic idea dates back at least to McTaggart's B-Theory of time, first published in *The Unreality of Time* in 1908, only three years after the first paper on relativity). This would mean that time is just another dimension, that future events are "already there", and that there is no objective flow of time. It is sometimes referred to as the "block time" or "block universe" theory due to its description of space-time as an unchanging four-dimensional "block", as opposed to the view of the world as a three-dimensional space modulated by the passage of time." Source: Wikipedia.

4   Self-Muscle testing: http://www.healing-with-eft.com/self-muscle-testing.html

5   Photos of self-muscle testing techniques: https://www.google.cl/imgres?imgurl=http://www.healing-with-eft.com/images/xFingerfinger-self-test.jpg.pagespeed.ic.GkDdwrB7WA.jpg&imgrefurl=http://www.healing-with-eft.com/self-muscle-testing.html&h=154&w=243&tbnid=iAwmjL2HtBymGM:&tbnh=154&tbnw=243&usg=__hnUUsDw4llUXgKXTc93UXmLYjtw%3D&vet=10ahUKEwjB-Niu-sjXAhVIHpAKHS4tAD8Q

9QEILzAA..i&docid=f9ffmwlVQBboDM&sa=X&ved=0ahUKEwjB-Niu-sjXAhVIHpA KHS4tAD8Q9QEILzAA.

6   YouTube of such an event: https://www.youtube.com/watch?v=RSLpiZgNlpA.

7   "An aura or Human energy field is according to New Age beliefs, a colored emanation said to enclose a human body or any animal or object. In some esoteric positions, the aura is described as a subtle body." Source: Wikipedia.
Richard Webster, *The Complete Book of Auras: Learn to See, Read, Strengthen & Heal Auras* (Woodberry: Llewellyn Publications, 2010).
Karla McLaren, *Your Aura & Your Chakras* (York Beach: Samuel Weiser, Inc, 1998).
Barbara Brennan, *Hands of Light.*
Rosalyn L. Bruyere, *Wheels of Light: Chakras, Auras, and the Healing Energy of the Body* (New York: Fireside, 1998).
Carol Ann Liaros and Kevin Todeschi, *Edgar Cayce on Auras and Colors: Learn to Understand Color and See Auras* (Virginia Beach: A.R.E. Press, 2011).

8   "Bioelectromagnetics, also known as bioelectromagnetism, is the study of the interaction between electromagnetic fields and biological entities. Areas of study include electrical or electromagnetic fields produced by living cells, tissues or organisms, including bioluminescent bacteria. Bioelectromagnetics: The term can also refer to the ability of living cells, tissues, and organisms to produce electrical fields and the response of cells to electromagnetic fields." Source: Wikipedia.

9   Dr. Hew Len, Hawaiian Psychologist, Using the Ho'ponopono, https://hubpages.com/religion-philosophy/How-Dr-Hew-Len-healed-a-ward-of-mentally-ill-criminals-with-Hooponopono.

10 Joe Vitale and Ihaleakala Hew Len, *Zero Limits: The Secret Hawaiian System for Wealth, Health, Peace and More.*

11 Oracle cards to check out: *I Can Do It Cards* by Louise Hay, *The Secret Language of Colour Cards* by Inna Segal, *Loving Words from Jesus* by Doreen Virtue, and *Ask Your Guides Oracle Cards* by Sonia Choquette.

12 Experiment in Finhorn, Scotland: https://www.findhorn.org.

13 Books on manifesting:
Katherine Hurst, *The Secret Law of Attraction: Master the Power of Intention.* (London: Greater Minds Ltd, 2016).
Joe Vitale, *Attractor Factor.*
Esther and Jerry Hicks, *Ask and It Is Given* (Hayhouse, 2004).
Barbel Mohr, *Cosmic Ordering Service* (Charlottesville: Hampton Roads Publishing, 2001).

14 Katherine Harmon, "Consequences for Newborns When Not Held," *Scientific America* (May 6, 2010).

15 Katherine Harmon, Consequences for Newborns when Not Held, *Paediatr Child Health*.15, no. 3 (March 2010): 153–156.

16 https://www.studyinnorway.no/living-in-norway/norwegian-society. http://www.everyculture.com/No-Sa/Norway.html.

17 Some examples of movies with unconditional love are *Titanic, Notebook, Hachi: A Dog's Tale, PS: I Love You,* and *City of Angels.*

18 Dr. Selye, *Stress without Distress.*

19 American Cancer Society, "Colon Cancer Cases Rising Among Young Adults," https://www.cancer.org/latest-news/colon-cancer-cases-rising-among-young-adults.html.

20 Dr. D'Adamo diet according to blood type experiments: *Eat Right 4 Your Type,* http://www.dadamo.com/typebase4/typebase5/T5.pl.

21 The amount of water in the body: https://en.wikipedia.org/wiki/Body_water.

22 The function of fats in the human body: www.eatbalanced.com.

23 Twelve foods that are high in omega-3: https://www.healthline.com/nutrition/12-omega-3-rich-foods#section8.

24 Dr. Michael Spira, *The 12 Minute Weight Loss Plan.*

25 "First 30 Seconds of an Interview," https://careerdirectionsllc.com/how-important-are-the-first-30-seconds-in-a-job-interview/. https://www.huffingtonpost.com/lisa-earle-mcleod/job-interview-tips_b_894670.html.

26 Robert Provine did experiments on the number of times adults and children laughed: http://mentalfloss.com/article/30329/lab-worlds-leading-laugh-scientist.
Another site on laughter: https://www.psychologytoday.com/blog/the-possibility-paradigm/201106/youre-not-laughing-enough-and-thats-no-joke.

27 "The butterfly effect is the concept that small causes can have large effects. Initially, it was used with weather prediction but later the term became a metaphor used in and out of science." Source: Wikipedia.

28 Skin recycle time: http://www.webmd.com/beauty/cosmetic-procedures-overview-skin#1.

29 Theoretical human life span is expected to be reached in sixty years' time: http://www.dailymail.co.uk/sciencetech/article-2802895/we-ll-soon-live-120-years-old-probably-absolute-limit-claims-expert.html.

CPSIA information can be obtained
at www.ICGtesting.com
Printed in the USA
BVHW03*0954030718
520736BV00003B/12/P